Creating an Investment Portfolio

Learn the available theories and their application

Partha Majumdar

ISBN-13: 9798863179643

Cover design by: Partha Majumdar

1 PREFACE

When I started earning in 1989, my salary was meager. However, my father made me invest in Insurance and Fixed/Recurring Deposits. I made my first investment in the Stock Market in 1994 by buying 2000 shares of Federal Lloyd Ltd for Rs. 20,000 from Bombay Stock Exchange (BSE). The process was cumbersome then as I had to invest through a Stockbroker in Calcutta, which my father introduced me to. The process of purchasing these shares took about one month before I had the Share Certificates. However, I have been investing in the Indian Stock Market ever since. Around 2000, I purchased my first Mutual Fund. I have continued to make systematic investments in Mutual Funds.

Investing in various instruments in India has become very easy in 2023. This has enhanced the number of investors. It is safe to say that most investors in India invest based on predefined notions and, more generally, on brokers' advice (including banks). That said, brokers' advice is important and should be considered. However, investing in any instrument requires reasonable research to make stable profits. The process becomes more intense when one needs to create a portfolio including various instruments.

There are many parameters to create a sound portfolio. This is because there are many investment instruments – each having its advantages & disadvantages and, more importantly, its utility. I have been experimenting with my investments and developing a few strategies.

I was assigned to create an investment strategy for a company in 2018. Instead of naming the company, I will refer to them as XYZ LLC. I suggested investing the corpus in Fixed Deposits, Mutual Funds, and Shares. This book details the process of arriving at the investment decisions. The various theories and calculations applied to arrive at the decisions are explained. As this report has no utility for XYZ LLC in 2023, I am making it available through this book in the hope that it can help make investment decisions for individuals and companies. It must be noted that while individuals must also consider other instruments like insurance, public/voluntary provident funds, instruments released by the government, real estate, etc., corporates must also consider instruments like options, derivatives, futures, real estate, etc. However, this book should give an idea for diversifying investments and optimizing for the goals.

Actual data of real companies have been used in this book to illustrate the concepts. I am making no recommendations regarding any company. The data is more than five years old and thus is not applicable in 2023. Also, there have been fundamental changes to many companies whose data is discussed in this book. The emphasis should be placed on understanding how a company's data needs to be analyzed.

Understanding and applying these techniques can make sound investment decisions and create a portfolio. I must make a disclaimer that actual profits realized from any strategy an individual uses depend on the understanding of the person and, ultimately, the will of the Almighty. One must appreciate that strategy or technique works differently for all two investors. Every investor needs to understand the strategy and apply their plan.

--- Partha Majumdar

Table of Contents

2   SETTING THE CONTEXT

XYZ LLC has set up a unit in India – XYZ India Pvt Ltd – in 2016. Initially, this unit was a pure cost center and thus depended on the mother company in Dubai for all its funds. However, with the development of XYZ India Pvt Ltd products, it generated revenue. Due to this revenue's presence, it has become essential for this money to be invested so that it does not lie idle; instead, it earns further income. This requirement is to create a plan for XYZ India Pvt Ltd to deploy funds in various instruments, including Fixed Deposits, Mutual Funds, and Shares.

XYZ needs a strategy so that the deployed funds can earn money, minimizing the involved risk. XYZ requires an asset allocation strategy between Fixed Deposits, Mutual Funds, and Shares to make maximum earnings from this portfolio at minimum risk.

The problem statement for XYZ LLC is to identify 5 Mutual Funds, between 6 to 10 Shares and up to 3 Fixed Deposit options to allocate a fund of Rs. 50,00,000 (Rupees Fifty Lakhs) such that this amount grows to the maximum possible amount within a time horizon of five years.

The scope of the Study is first to determine an asset allocation strategy between Fixed Deposits, Mutual Funds, and Shares for a total corpus of Rs. 50,00,000. To do so, **we will calculate the**

utility of the returns from the investment for the Investor as per the **risk appetite** of the Investor.

We will consider two types of Fixed Deposits for study – Fixed Deposits in large Bank in India (We will consider this to be Risk-Free Investment) and Fixed Deposits in Cooperative Banks (We will consider this to be a risky investment as is the case and this also provide much higher returns as compared to Fixed Deposits with Nationalized Bank or Large Private Bank in India).

After the asset allocation between Fixed Deposits, Mutual Funds, and Shares (We will refer to these as **Asset Classes**), the scope of the study is to determine asset allocation within each Asset Class. In other words, once we have identified 5 Mutual Funds to invest in, we will determine the best allocation of funds to the Mutual Fund Asset Class to each of the Mutual Funds so that the risk is minimized and the returns are maximized. The same will be done for Fixed Deposits and Shares.

In the case of Fixed Deposits and Mutual Funds, it is possible to create a plan upfront for the next five years. However, **in the case of Shares, it is only prudent to plan upfront for one year**. So, this study will be restricted to determining the shares to invest in the first year and will provide the different algorithms to apply for the subsequent years.

3 METHODOLOGY

There are six parts to this study. They are as follows:

1. Allocation of funds to the different Asset Classes. The Asset Classes are Fixed Deposits in Large Indian Banks, Fixed Deposits in Cooperative Banks, Mutual Funds, and Shares.

2. Allocation of Funds allocated to the Fixed Deposit Asset Class between the different Fixed Deposits, i.e., Fixed Deposits in Large Indian Banks and Fixed Deposits in Cooperative Banks.

3. The strategy to be used to select Mutual Funds to be invested in.

4. Allocations of Funds allocated to Mutual Fund Asset Class between the five Mutual Funds chosen for Investment.

5. The strategy to be used for selecting Shares to be invested in.

6. Allocation of Funds allocated to Shares Asset Class between 6 to 10 Shares chosen for Investment.

We will adopt a different methodology for these six cases stated above. These six methodologies are stated below.

3.1 METHODOLOGY FOR ALLOCATION OF FUNDS BETWEEN ASSET CLASSES

We need to determine the portfolio in which funds are allocated between Fixed Deposits, Mutual Funds, and Shares so that the Risk is minimum and the Returns are maximum.

3.1.1 RISK

We will measure Risk in terms of the Standard Deviation of the Returns from the Asset Class.

We will consider investment in Fixed Deposits in Large Banks in India as Risk-Free (or Zero Risk).

We will gather the returns from these investments over the past five years for Fixed Deposits in Cooperative Banks. We will take the Standard Deviation of these Returns to determine the Risk in Investment in Fixed Deposits in Cooperative Banks.

For Mutual Funds, a Probabilistic Model will be created based on inputs from three Investment Bankers. The Probabilistic Model will state the probability of Returns in Mutual Funds in Good Times and Bad Times. Based on this, the Risk of Investment in Mutual Funds will be determined.

For Shares, the NIFTY Index will be gathered from 01-Jan-2017 to 31-May-2018. The Standard Deviation of the NIFTY Index over this period would be considered as the Risk in Share Investment.

3.1.2 RETURNS

For Fixed Deposits (both from Large Indian Banks and Cooperative Banks), we will consider the current rate of return as the rate of return.

For Mutual Funds and Shares, we will take inputs from three Investment Bankers regarding their projection of Returns from the Market in Good Times and Bad Times. Based on this, a Probabilistic Model will be created to determine the returns from Mutual Funds and Shares (separately).

3.1.3 ASSET ALLOCATION

As a strategy, to ensure that the portfolio is well diversified, we will ensure that we do not allocate more than 40% in any one Asset Class.

We will make an initial allocation between the Asset Classes. From this allocation, we will get the Expected Returns from the Portfolio and the Risk (Standard Deviation). From this, we will compute the Utility of the Investment for the Investor using the formula as follows:

$$\textbf{Utility = E(R) − (}^1/_2\textbf{) * (A) * (V)}$$

Where, E(R) is the Expected Returns, A is the Coefficient of Risk Aversion, and V is the Variance.

Then, to distribute the corpus between the different Asset Classes, we will set up a Linear Programming Problem so that the Utility from the Portfolio is maximized for the Risk Appetite of the Investor.

To solve the Linear Programming problem, we will use **Solver** in **Excel**.

3.2 METHODOLOGY FOR ALLOCATION OF FUNDS WITHIN FIXED DEPOSITS ASSET CLASS

We will consider Fixed Deposits in Large Indian Banks to be Risk-Free.

We have seen that the Reserve Bank of India (RBI) has been reducing the REPO Rate for the last four years or keeping it unchanged. Only after four consecutive years RBI increased the REPO Rate in June 2018 by 0.25%. Experts feel that RBI could raise the REPO Rate one more time before the next General Elections in 2019.

Seeing the current Indian Scenario, we will speculate that the present BJP Government will be voted to power in 2019. Under this assumption, we will consider that the current Government Policies will be continued. Under those circumstances, it is likely, with the recent Economic Indicators, there is significantly less possibility for the REPO Rate to be increased by RBI.

This assumption is essential for our methodology for investing in Fixed Deposits as we will invest for the long term at the very beginning to avoid facing a situation for reduced Return rates from Fixed Deposit in the future.

So, we will adopt the methodology that we will invest in Fixed Deposit for five years or more at the current rate of return. The current rate of return from Large Indian Banks can be obtained from their website. The current rate of return from the Cooperative Banks will be determined by visiting the bank and getting this information.

Further, as the company has an account in HDFC Bank Ltd, we will consider investment in Fixed Deposit in a Large Indian Bank to be in HDFC Bank Ltd. For the investment in Fixed Deposit in Cooperative Bank, we will consider investing in Ananda Cooperative Bank and Gnana Shale Souharda Cooperative Bank. The choice of Gnana Shale Souharda Cooperative Bank is because the company interacts with this Bank for all stamp paper requirements and thus can closely watch this Bank. As for Ananda Cooperative Bank, the office of this bank is right next to the company's offices. **Investing in two cooperative banks will reduce the risk as it will provide for diversification**.

We will find the Standard Deviation of the Fixed Deposit Portfolio to determine the allocation. We will consider this to be a 2-asset portfolio with one asset being Fixed Deposit in Large Indian Banks (Risk-Free) and one asset being Fixed Deposits in Cooperative Banks (Risky).

We will consider the Correlation between the Fixed Deposits in Large Indian Banks and Fixed Deposits in Cooperative Banks as 1. This is because the interest rate on both types of Fixed Deposits will always move in the same direction whenever the REPO rate changes from RBI.

We will solve the Linear Programming Problem for minimizing the Standard Deviation (or Risk) to find the allocation in the 2-asset portfolio.

To solve the Linear Programming problem, we will use **Solver** in **Excel**.

3.3 METHODOLOGY FOR SELECTING MUTUAL FUNDS TO INVEST IN

One of the main objectives for selecting Mutual Funds for the portfolio is to ensure that we have a well-diversified set of Mutual Funds to minimize risk. We will diversify the Mutual Fund portfolio from various points of view.

3.3.1 INDEX MUTUAL FUND

The first criteria for diversification will be between Funds based on the Index and Funds not based on the Index (or managed by Fund Managers). As our investment horizon is five years, investing in these types of Mutual Funds is essential. It is generally observed that Index Based Mutual Funds outperform the Funds managed by Fund Managers over eight years. **Research shows there is only a 2% chance that a Mutual Fund managed by a Fund Manager will beat an index-based Mutual Fund after eight years of investment**.

As we must select five Mutual Funds, we will keep one Mutual Fund as an Index Fund. We will study at least two Index Mutual Funds and choose one from this set.

To study the Index Mutual Funds, we will gather the Returns from the Index Mutual Funds over the last five years. From this data, we will compute the Average Returns as of date. This will be the Return on Asset from the Index Mutual Fund value.

We can compute the Standard Deviation of the Index Mutual Fund from the returns data. This will provide the component of risk involved in the Index Mutual Fund.

Using the value from Return on Asset and Standard Deviation, we can compute the Sharpe Ratio for the Index Mutual Fund using the following formula.

Sharpe Ratio = (Return on Asset – Risk-Free Rate) **/** (Standard Deviation)

The Returns from Fixed Deposits in Large Indian Banks will be considered the Risk-Free Rate.

The Index Mutual Fund with the <u>highest Sharpe Ratio</u> will make it to our Portfolio of Mutual Funds.

3.3.2 MUTUAL FUND MANAGED BY FUND MANAGERS

Regarding selecting Mutual Funds managed by Fund Managers, we will create two types: Mutual Funds primarily invested in Equities and Mutual Funds invested in Debt instruments.

We will study the recommendations available on the Economic Times website for selecting the Mutual Fund primarily invested in Debt instruments. **We will choose ONE Debt Fund, which has the highest Sharpe Ratio**.

We will have to select three more Mutual Funds, which will be Mutual Funds primarily invested in Equities. For choosing the three Equity-based Mutual Funds, we will study at least five Equity-based Mutual Funds. We will compute the **G-Score** and **F-Score** for all these Mutual Funds. We will consider the top 50 percentiles of these

21

equity-based Mutual Funds for further selection. **Among the equity-based Mutual Funds in the top 50 percentiles, we will choose the set of three Mutual Funds that are most diversified as per the correlations between the returns of the Funds**.

G-Score was formulated by Professor Mohandas. It is applicable for the Growth Shares.

Calculating G-Score

G-Score is an integer value between 0 and 8.

Companies with higher G-Scores are favorable for investment.

To calculate the G-Score, we need to consider the following eight aspects of a Company and assign a score of 0 or 1 as per the criteria provided below for each aspect. Then, we sum up the scores of all the eight aspects to arrive at the G-Score for the Company.

The eight aspects and the criteria are provided below.

Sl.	Aspect	How to calculate	Scoring Criteria
G1	Earnings return on assets	(Net income before extraordinary items) / (Average Total Assets for last 2 Years)	Assign 1 if value is greater than Industry Median; otherwise assign 0

G2	Cashflow return on assets	(Cash from Operations) / (Average Total Assets for last 2 Years)	Assign 1 if value is greater than Industry Median; otherwise assign 0
G3	Accruals	Gather figures for Cash from Operations (CFO) and Net Income (NI)	If CFO > NI, assign 1; otherwise assign 0
G4	Stability of earnings	Find Variance of Company's quarterly earnings return on assets over the last 4 years	Assign 0 if value is greater than Industry Median; otherwise assign 1
G5	Sales Growth variability	Find Variance of a Company's quarterly growth of sales over the last 4 years	Assign 0 if value is greater than Industry Median; otherwise assign 1
G6	R & D intensity	(Amount Spent on R&D in this Year) / (Total Assets at the beginning of the Year)	Assign 1 if value is greater than Industry Median; otherwise assign 0
G7	Capital expenditure intensity	(Amount Spent on Capital Expenditure in this Year) / (Total Assets at the beginning of the Year)	Assign 1 if value is greater than Industry Median; otherwise assign 0
G8	Advertising expense intensity	(Amount Spent on Advertising in this Year) / (Total Assets at the beginning of the Year)	Assign 1 if value is greater than Industry Median; otherwise assign 0

F-Score was formulated by Piotroski. It is applicable for all the Value Shares.

Calculating F-Score

F-Score is an integer value between 0 and 9.

Companies with higher F-Scores are favorable for investment.

To calculate the F-Score, we need to consider the following nine aspects of a Company and assign a score of 0 or 1 as per the criteria provided below for each aspect. Then, we sum up the scores of all the nine aspects to arrive at the F-Score for the Company.

The nine aspects and the criteria are provided below.

Sl.	Aspect	How to calculate	Scoring Criteria
F1	Return on Assets (ROA)	(Net Income before extraordinary items) / (Total Assets at the beginning of the year)	Assign 1 if ROA is > 0; otherwise assign 0
F2	Cashflow from Operations (CFO)	(Cash from Operations) / (Total Assets at the beginning of the year)	Assign 1 if CFO > 0; otherwise assign 0
F3	ΔROA	Current Year's ROA – Previous Years ROA	If ΔROA > 0, assign 1; otherwise assign 0
F4	Accrual	ROA = (Net income before extraordinary items) / (Total Assets at the beginning of the year)	Assign 1 if CFO > ROA; otherwise assign 0

		CFO = (Cash from Operations) / (Total Assets at the beginning of the year)	
F5	ΔLeverage	(Current Year Long-Term Debts / Average Total Assets for the last 2 years) – (Previous Year Long-Term Debts / Average Total Assets for the last 2 years)	Assign 0 if value is greater than 0; otherwise assign 1
F6	ΔLiquid	(Current Ratio for the Current Year) – (Current Ratio for the Previous Year) Current Ratio = (Current Assets) / (Current Liabilities)	Assign 1 if value is greater 0; otherwise assign 0
F7	Equity Capital	(Amount of Equity offered in the Current Year)	Assign 1 if value is less than or equal to 0; otherwise assign 1
F8	ΔMargin	(Gross Margin Ratio for Current Year) - (Gross Margin Ratio for Previous Year) Gross Margin Ratio = (Gross Margin) / (Total Sales)	Assign 1 if value is greater than 0; otherwise assign 0
F9	ΔTurnover	(Asset Turnover Ratio for Current Year) – (Asset Turnover Ratio for Previous Year) Asset Turnover Ratio = (Total Sales) / (Total Assets at the beginning of the Year)	Assign 1 if value is greater than 0; otherwise assign 0

We will gather the information regarding which shares the Equity-Based Mutual Fund is invested in. From this information, we will collect which investments are investment in Growth Shares and which are in Value Shares. <u>The Shares with high Price-to-Book value will be considered as Growth Shares. The Shares with low Price-to-Book value will be regarded as Value Shares</u>.

For all the Growth Shares, we will compute the G-Score.

For all the Value Shares, we will compute the F-Score.

We will take a weighted average of the G-Score and F-Score for an Equity-Based Mutual Fund to arrive at the Score for the Mutual Fund.

Score for Mutual Fund = (%age Investment in Growth Shares * G-Score) + (%age Investment in Value Shares * F-Score)

3.4 METHODOLOGY FOR ALLOCATION OF FUNDS WITHIN MUTUAL FUND ASSET CLASS

Once the Mutual Funds to be invested in have been identified, we will find the Returns from these Mutual Funds over the last five years or more. This data will give us the Average Returns from the Mutual funds. **We will use the Average Returns over the previous five or more years as the <u>Return on Assets</u> from the Mutual Fund**.

Next, we will study the portfolio of each Mutual Fund. We will get the values of the weights in each Equity that the Mutual Fund has invested in. Also, for each of the Equity, we can get the value of β(**Beta)** for the Equity. Using the values of β for the individual Equities, **we can compute the value of β for the Portfolio as the weighted sum of the individual β.**

$$\beta_{Portfolio} = w_1 * \beta_1 + w_2 * \beta_2 + ... + w_n * \beta_n$$

where β_1, β_2, ..., β_n is the β for the individual equities and w_1, w_2, ..., w_n are the corresponding weights of allocations in these equities.

Using the values of Expected Returns and β, we can compute the **Treynor Ratio** for the Portfolio. The Treynor Ratio can be calculated using the formula given below.

$$\text{Treynor Ratio} = \frac{(\text{Return on Asset} - \text{Risk Free Rate})}{\beta}$$

The Returns from Fixed Deposits in Large Indian Banks will be considered the Risk-Free Rate.

We will set up a Linear Programming problem for finding the Asset Allocation in each Mutual Fund to maximize the Treynor Ratio.

To solve the Linear Programming problem, we will use **Solver** in Excel.

3.5 METHODOLOGY FOR SELECTING SHARES TO INVEST IN

We cannot select stocks (shares) where we can stay invested for five years and expect returns. We will start with some purchases using a few strategies and then short (sell) and long (buy) based on various strategies.

For selecting Shares for investment, we will apply three different strategies. These strategies are as follows.

1. Using SUE Score.

2. Using Sloan's Method.

3. Using Pairs Trading Strategy.

Each method is explained below.

3.5.1 SUE SCORE METHOD

SUE is the acronym for **Standardized Unexpected Earning**.

$$\text{SUE Score} = \text{(Actual EPS – Expected EPS)} / \text{(Standard Deviation of EPS)}$$

- **EPS stands for Earning Per Share.**

- **Actual EPS** is the current EPS released in the last year's Financial Statements.

- **Expected EPS** is calculated by finding the Average of the EPS at the end of the last four years (before the current year).

- **Standard Deviation of EPS** is calculated by finding the Standard Deviation of the last four year's EPS.

After finding the SUE Score of the Stocks of interest, order them in the descending order of the SUE Score.

As a thumb rule, we will sell all Stocks with a negative SUE Score.

Also, we will consider selling all Stocks with a very low SUE Score.

We will consider buying the Stock with the highest SUE Scores (positive values only).

3.5.1.1   HOW LONG DO YOU STAY INVESTED?

After investing in the Shares chosen through SUE Score, we will stay invested in the Shares for a minimum period of one year.

3.5.2 SLOAN'S METHOD

Richard G. Sloan had written a paper in 1996 for a trading strategy. This paper has shown that this strategy made profits for 28 out of 30 continuous years. This strategy is beneficial for trading in the Indian markets today.

The strategy is that we need to consider the amount of accruals in a company and not just the total revenue. The strategy states that companies with more earnings from accruals will eventually generate lower profits for stock traders than those with higher cash equivalents and lower accruals.

The strategy's rationale is that accruals may or may not convert into cash. This can happen because of accidents where the company fails to collect its dues from the services and products rendered. Also, it can be due to the company's internal strategies to reflect better numbers to the traders.

One example of how accruals can be manufactured is from the automobile industry. The delivery managers generally push finished inventory to the distributors without firm orders. This immediately inflates the current receivables and thus increases the company's assets. However, these are accruals and may not convert into cash. There is every likelihood that the Distributors may not be able to sell the inventory and return it to the manufacturer.

So, Sloan's method is to find out the actual cash equivalent of a company and make decisions to buy or sell stocks based on that.

Sloan's formula is calculated as follows:

Step 1: Calculate the Accruals (Let us call this "A")

To calculate the accruals, the below formula needs to be used.

$$
\begin{aligned}
\text{Accruals} = \ & (\Delta\text{Current Assets} - \Delta\text{Cash}) \\
& - (\Delta\text{Current Liabilities} - \Delta\text{Total Short Term Debts} - \Delta\text{Tax Payable}) \\
& - \text{Depreciation}
\end{aligned}
$$

Here,

- ☐ ΔCurrent Assets = Current Assets of Current Year – Current Assets of Previous Year

- ☐ ΔCash = Cash of Current Year – Current Cash of Previous Year

- ☐ ΔCurrent Liabilities = Current Liabilities of Current Year – Current Liabilities of Previous Year

- ☐ ΔTotal Short-Term Debts = Total Short-Term Debts of Current Year – Total Short-Term Debts of Previous Year

- ☐ ΔTax Payable = Tax Payable of Current Year – Tax Payable of Previous Year

- ☐ Depreciation is taken for the Current Year.

Step 2: Determine the Total Income from Continuous Operations (Let us call this "I")

This can be determined from the Income Statement of the Company. Some companies also call this a "Statement of Profit and Loss."

Step 3: Calculate Sloan Score = (I – A) / (Average Assets of Current Year and Previous Year)

The higher the Sloan Score, the Stock should be bought (or go long on the Stock). The lower the Sloan Score, the stock should be sold (or short it).

3.5.2.1　HOW LONG DO YOU STAY INVESTED?

After investing in the Shares chosen through Sloan's Method, we will stay invested in the Shares for a minimum period of one year.

3.5.3 PAIRS TRADING STRATEGY

"Pairs Strategy" is a short-term speculation Strategy. "Pair Trading" is, in essence, a Contrarian Investment Strategy. "Pairs Trading" is a medium-term Trading Strategy.

3.5.3.1　The Strategy

1. Find two Stocks whose prices have moved together for an extended period.
2. When the spread between them widens, short the Winner and long the Loser.

3.5.3.1.1　How do we identify the Stocks that move together?

1. Observe the stock prices over 12 months. **This period of observation is called the FORMATION PERIOD.**
2. Construct a Cumulative Returns Index for each Stock over the Formation Period.
3. Choose a Matching Partner for each Stock by finding one that minimizes the sum of squared deviations between the 2 Normalized Prices. *(Normalized Prices can be found by using a*

method like taking each Stock Price and subtracting the Mean of the Stock Prices over the observation period and then dividing this difference by the Standard Deviation of the Stock Prices over the observation period).

3.5.3.1.2   How far do the Stocks in the Pair have to Diverge before we can apply this Strategy?

When the Stock Prices of the Stocks in the Pair diverge by more than 2 Standard Deviations, we start the **TRADING PERIOD**. *(The Trading Period must be six months).*

3.5.3.1.3   When should we unwind the position?

- We should unwind the position at the point where the Stock Prices of the Pair cross each other.
- If the Stock Prices of Pair do not cross during the Trading Period, we unwind on the last day.
- If one of the Stocks in the Pair is delisted, then we close the position in the Pair.

3.5.3.2   Why should this Strategy earn returns?

By shorting the Winner and buying the Loser, if history repeats itself, the prices will converge, and the arbitrageur will profit.

3.5.3.3 How to reduce Risk on the Portfolio through this Strategy?

After using the strategy, the risk can be reduced by increasing the number of pairs selected for trading. As the number of Pairs in the Portfolio increases, the portfolio Standard Deviation falls. Also, it is noticed that as the number of Pairs in the Portfolio increases, the minimum realized returns increase while the maximum realized excess returns remain relatively stable.

3.5.3.4 What are the observed returns from this Strategy?

For formulating this strategy, the researchers have studied data from the US Market between 1962 and 2002. They have found that adopting this strategy can yield 11% excess returns.

3.5.3.5 HOW LONG DO YOU STAY INVESTED?

After investing in the Shares chosen through the Pairs Strategy, we will stay invested in the Shares for a maximum period of six months.

3.6 METHODOLOGY FOR ALLOCATION OF FUNDS WITHIN SHARES ASSET CLASS

The amount allocated to Shares and each Share will depend on the risk the person can take. So, we will get a measure of the risk the investor is willing to take. The measure of risk in Shares can be defined by the β of the Share. Once we have the β for individual Shares, we can compute the β for the portfolio as follows.

$$\beta_{Portfolio} = w_1 * \beta_1 + w_2 * \beta_2 + ... + w_n * \beta_n$$

where $\beta_1, \beta_2, ..., \beta_n$ is the β for the individual Share and $w_1, w_2, ..., w_n$ are the corresponding weights of allocations in these Shares.

To allocate funds in each Share, we will form a Linear Programming problem such that the value of β is maximized within the upper limit for the β the investor is ready to undertake.

To solve the Linear Programming problem, we will use **Solver** in Excel.

4 SOURCE DATA

The source data is obtained from www.economictimes.com,
www.bseindia.com, www.nseindia.com and
www.moneycontrol.com.

Apart from this, we will scan the Internet for the Annual Reports of
various companies. The list of the companies whose Annual Reports
are studied is provided in **Appendix I**.

5 APPLYING A MODEL FOR ASSET ALLOCATION BETWEEN ASSET CLASSES

We must consider three Asset Classes – Fixed Deposits, Mutual Funds, and Shares. To determine the allocation of funds between these Asset Classes, we first need to define the Returns and Risks in each Asset Class.

We define the Risk and Return for each Asset Class one by one.

We then define the correlation between the three asset classes.

Lastly, before applying the model and allocating the funds between the asset classes, we will define the Coefficient of Risk Aversion for the Investor.

5.1 RISK

We will calculate the risk involved in the instruments.

5.1.1 FIXED DEPOSIT

The first instrument for which we will compute the risk is the fixed deposits.

5.1.1.1   INDIVIDUAL STANDARD DEVIATIONS

We will consider investing in Fixed deposits for the following institutions.

1. **HDFC Bank Ltd.**: This is a Large Indian Bank. We will consider investment in Fixed Deposit in this Bank as Risk-Free. The Interest Rates provided by this bank over the last five years are as follows.

Year →	2018	2017	2016	2015	2014
Average Rate of Interest	7.10%	6.80%	6.50%	7.00%	7.90%

We see that there has been variation in Interest Rates over the last five years. However, we consider that the Bank will return this interest. **Thus, we will consider the Risk in Investment in HDFC Bank Ltd as 0%**.

We will denote HDFC Bank Ltd by **H**.

We will denote the Standard Deviation or Risk from Investment in Fixed Deposit in HDFC Bank Ltd as σ_H.

So, $\sigma_H = 0$.

2. **Ananda Cooperative Bank**: This is a Cooperative Bank. We will consider investment in Fixed Deposit in this Bank as Risky. The Interest Rates provided by this bank over the last five years are as follows.

Year →	2018	2017	2016	2015	2014
Average Rate of Interest	8.50%	9.00%	9.00%	9.50%	10.00%

The Standard Deviation of these Interest Rates is <u>0.57%</u>. We will consider this to be the risk in this Instrument. *(Though it must be said that this is not an appropriate measure of this risk).*

We will denote Ananda Cooperative Bank by **A**.

We will denote the Standard Deviation or Risk from Investment in Fixed Deposit in Ananda Cooperative Bank as σ_A.

So, σ_A = 0.57%.

3. **Gnana Shale Souharda Cooperative Bank**: This is a Cooperative Bank. We will consider investment in Fixed Deposit in this Bank as Risky. The Interest Rates provided by this bank over the last five years are as follows.

Year →	2018	2017	2016	2015	2014
Average Rate of Interest	11.50%	13.00%	13.00%	13.50%	14.50%

The Standard Deviation of these Interest Rates is <u>1.08%</u>. We will consider this to be the risk in this Instrument. *(Though it must be said that this is not an appropriate measure of this risk).*

We will denote Gnana Shale Souharda Cooperative Bank by **G**.

We will denote the Standard Deviation or Risk from Investment in Fixed Deposit in Gnana Shale Souharda Cooperative Bank as σ_G.

So, σ_G = 1.08%.

5.1.1.2   CORRELATIONS

From the above Interest Rates over the last five years, we can determine the correlations between these three Banks. Correlation between two instruments, X and Y, can be found using the following formula.

Correlation(X,Y) = Covariance(X,Y) / (σ_X * σ_Y),

where σ_X is the Standard Deviation of X and σ_Y is the Standard Deviation of Y.

So, the correlation table between the three banks is as follows.

	H	A	G
H	1.00		
A	0.53	1.00	
G	0.41	0.78	1.00

So, Correlation(H, A) = ρ_{HA}▯▯▯▯▯▯▯

Correlation(H, G) = ρ_{HG}▯▯▯▯▯▯▯

Correlation(A, G) = ρ_{AG}▯▯▯▯▯▯▯

5.1.1.3   RISK FROM FIXED DEPOSITS

To find the risk from Fixed Deposits, we will initially assume that we will allocate an equal amount into Fixed Deposits in HDFC Bank Ltd, Ananda Cooperative Bank, and Gnana Shale Souharda Cooperative Bank. In other words, we will consider that the weights of investment in the Fixed Deposits in the three Banks, w_H, w_A, and w_G, all equal 33.33%.

With this assumption, we can find the Standard Deviation of the Fixed Deposit Portfolio (σ_P) as follows.

$$\sigma_P = w_H{}^2 * \sigma_H{}^2 + w_A{}^2 * \sigma_A{}^2 + w_G{}^2 * \sigma_G{}^2 + 2 * \rho_{HA} * w_H * w_A * \sigma_H * \sigma_A + 2 * \rho_{HG} * w_H * w_G * \sigma_H * \sigma_G + 2 * w_A * w_G * \rho_{AG} * \sigma_A * \sigma_G$$

Using this formula, we get the risk for the portfolio as follows.

$$\sigma_P = 2.73 * 10^{-5}$$

So, we can consider the Risk from Investment in Fixed Deposits as 0.

5.1.2 MUTUAL FUNDS

To figure out the Risk and Return from Mutual Funds, I consulted three Investment Bankers. They are:-

1. Mr. S (C1)
2. Mr. R (C2)

3. Mr. D (C3)

The names and the companies of the consultants have been obfuscated.

From them, I got the following figures regarding the possible returns from Mutual Funds.

Consultant	OPTIMISTIC RETURNS		PESSIMISTIC RETURNS	
	Probability	Return	Probability	Return
C1	70%	20%	30%	5%
C2	60%	22%	40%	5%
C3	60%	18%	40%	8%

From these figures, we can calculate the Returns as predicted by each of the Consultants.

Consultant	Calculation for Return	Return
C1	70% * 20% + 30% * 5%	15.50%
C2	60% * 22% + 40% * 5%	15.20%
C3	60% * 18% + 40% * 8%	14.00%
AVERAGE RETURN PREDICTED		14.90%

Now, we can calculate the Risk from the Mutual Funds as predicted by these three consultants. <u>Note that Risk is measured as Standard Deviation. Standard Deviation is the SQUARE ROOT of Variance</u>.

Consultant	Calculation for Variance	Risk
C1	70% * (20% - 15.5%)^2 + 30% * (5% - 15.5%)^2	6.87%
C2	60% * (22% - 15.2%)^2 + 40% * (5% - 15.2%)^2	8.33%
C3	60% * (18% - 14%)^2 + 40% * (8% - 14%)^2	4.90%
AVERAGE RISK PREDICTED		6.70%

So, we will consider the Risk from Investment in Mutual Funds as 6.70%.

5.1.3 SHARES

To determine the Risk involved in Shares, we will find the Standard Deviation of the NIFTY Index from 01-Jan-2017 to 31-May-2018.

The NIFTY Index Data gathered is provided below.

	2017											
	Jan	Feb	Mar	Apr	May	Jun	Jul	Aug	Sep	Oct	Nov	Dec
1	8,185.80	8,716.40	8,945.80	9,173.75	9,304.05	9,616.10	9,520.90	10,114.65	9,974.40	9,788.60	10,440.50	10,121.80
2	8,179.50	8,734.25	8,899.75	9,173.75	9,313.80	9,653.50	9,520.90	10,081.50	9,974.40	9,788.60	10,423.80	10,121.80
3	8,192.25	8,740.95	8,897.55	9,237.85	9,311.95	9,653.50	9,615.00	10,013.65	9,974.40	9,859.50	10,452.50	10,121.80
4	8,190.50	8,740.95	8,897.55	9,237.85	9,359.90	9,653.50	9,613.30	10,066.40	9,912.85	9,914.90	10,452.50	10,127.75
5	8,273.80	8,740.95	8,897.55	9,265.15	9,285.30	9,675.10	9,637.60	10,066.40	9,952.20	9,888.70	10,452.50	10,118.25
6	8,243.80	8,801.05	8,963.45	9,261.95	9,285.30	9,637.15	9,674.55	10,066.40	9,916.20	9,979.70	10,451.80	10,044.10
7	8,243.80	8,768.30	8,946.90	9,198.30	9,285.30	9,663.90	9,665.80	10,057.40	9,929.90	9,979.70	10,350.15	10,166.70
8	8,243.80	8,769.05	8,924.30	9,198.30	9,314.05	9,647.25	9,665.80	9,978.55	9,934.80	9,979.70	10,303.15	10,265.65
9	8,236.05	8,778.40	8,927.00	9,198.30	9,316.85	9,668.25	9,665.80	9,908.05	9,934.80	9,988.75	10,308.95	10,265.65
10	8,288.60	8,793.55	8,934.55	9,181.45	9,407.30	9,668.25	9,771.05	9,820.25	9,934.80	10,016.95	10,321.75	10,265.65
11	8,380.65	8,793.55	8,934.55	9,237.00	9,422.40	9,668.25	9,786.05	9,710.80	10,006.05	9,984.80	10,321.75	10,322.25
12	8,407.20	8,793.55	8,934.55	9,203.45	9,400.90	9,616.40	9,816.10	9,710.80	10,093.05	10,096.40	10,321.75	10,240.15
13	8,400.35	8,805.05	8,934.55	9,150.80	9,400.90	9,606.90	9,891.70	9,710.80	10,079.30	10,167.45	10,224.95	10,192.95
14	8,400.35	8,792.30	9,087.00	9,150.80	9,400.90	9,618.15	9,886.35	9,794.15	10,086.60	10,167.45	10,186.60	10,252.10
15	8,400.35	8,724.70	9,084.80	9,150.80	9,445.40	9,578.05	9,886.35	9,794.15	10,085.40	10,167.45	10,118.05	10,333.25
16	8,412.80	8,778.00	9,153.70	9,150.80	9,512.25	9,588.05	9,886.35	10,085.40	10,085.40	10,230.85	10,214.75	10,333.25
17	8,398.00	8,821.70	9,160.05	9,139.30	9,525.75	9,588.05	9,915.95	9,904.15	10,085.40	10,234.45	10,283.60	10,333.25
18	8,417.00	8,821.70	9,160.05	9,105.15	9,429.45	9,588.05	9,827.15	9,837.40	10,153.10	10,210.85	10,283.60	10,388.75
19	8,100.10	8,001.70	8,100.00	8,100.00	8,127.50	8,007.00	8,000.00	8,001.40	10,147.55	10,140.55	10,203.00	10,403.20
20	8,349.35	8,879.20	9,126.85	9,136.40	9,427.90	9,653.50	9,873.30	9,837.40	10,141.15	10,146.55	10,298.75	10,444.20
21	8,349.35	8,907.85	9,121.50	9,119.40	9,427.90	9,633.60	9,915.25	9,754.35	10,121.90	10,146.55	10,326.90	10,440.30
22	8,349.35	8,926.90	9,030.45	9,119.40	9,438.25	9,630.00	9,915.25	9,765.55	9,964.40	10,146.55	10,342.30	10,493.00
23	8,391.50	8,939.50	9,086.30	9,119.40	9,386.15	9,574.95	9,915.25	9,852.50	9,964.40	10,184.85	10,348.75	10,493.00
24	8,475.80	8,939.50	9,108.00	9,217.95	9,360.55	9,574.95	9,966.40	9,857.05	9,964.40	10,207.70	10,389.70	10,493.00
25	8,602.75	8,939.50	9,108.00	9,306.60	9,509.75	9,574.95	9,964.55	9,857.05	9,872.60	10,295.35	10,389.70	10,493.00
26	8,602.75	8,939.50	9,108.00	9,351.85	9,595.10	9,574.95	10,020.65	9,857.05	9,871.50	10,343.80	10,389.70	10,531.50
27	8,641.25	8,896.70	9,045.20	9,342.15	9,595.10	9,511.40	10,020.55	9,857.05	9,735.75	10,323.05	10,399.55	10,490.75
28	8,641.25	8,879.60	9,100.80	9,304.05	9,595.10	9,491.25	10,014.50	9,912.80	9,768.95	10,323.05	10,370.25	10,477.90
29	8,641.25		9,143.80	9,304.05	9,604.90	9,504.10	10,014.50	9,796.05	9,788.60	10,323.05	10,361.30	10,530.70
30	8,632.75		9,173.75	9,304.05	9,624.55	9,520.90	10,014.50	9,884.40	9,788.60	10,363.65	10,226.55	10,530.70
31	8,561.30		9,173.75		9,621.25		10,077.10	9,917.90		10,335.30		10,530.70

	2018											
	Jan	Feb	Mar	Apr	May	Jun	Jul	Aug	Sep	Oct	Nov	Dec
1	10,435.55	11,019.35	10,458.35	10,113.70	10,739.35							
2	10,442.20	10,760.60	10,458.35	10,211.80	10,716.95							
3	10,443.20	10,760.60	10,458.35	10,243.05	10,668.50							
4	10,504.80	10,760.60	10,458.35	10,120.20	10,618.25							
5	10,558.85	10,666.55	10,358.85	10,328.95	10,618.25							
6	10,558.85	10,498.25	10,221.20	10,331.60	10,618.25							
7	10,558.85	10,476.70	10,163.55	10,331.60	10,715.50							
8	10,623.60	10,576.85	10,242.65	10,331.60	10,717.80							
9	10,637.00	10,454.95	10,226.85	10,379.35	10,741.70							
10	10,632.20	10,454.95	10,226.85	10,401.05	10,715.55							
11	10,651.20	10,454.95	10,226.85	10,417.15	10,806.50							
12	10,681.25	10,533.70	10,422.70	10,458.65	10,806.50							
13	10,681.25	10,539.75	10,426.85	10,480.60	10,806.50							
14	10,681.25	10,500.90	10,410.90	10,480.60	10,806.60							
15	10,761.50	10,545.50	10,360.15	10,480.60	10,801.85							
16	10,700.45	10,452.30	10,195.15	10,528.35	10,741.10							
17	10,788.55	10,452.30	10,195.15	10,548.70	10,682.70							
18	10,817.00	10,452.30	10,195.15	10,526.20	10,599.50							
19	10,894.70	10,378.40	10,094.20	10,565.30	10,596.40							
20	10,894.70	10,360.40	10,136.55	10,564.05	10,596.40							
21	10,894.70	10,397.49	10,155.25	10,564.05	10,521.05							
22	10,966.20	10,382.70	10,155.25	10,564.05	10,536.70							
23	11,069.35	10,491.05	9,998.05	10,584.70	10,429.05							
24	11,086.00	10,491.05	9,998.05	10,617.75	10,528.80							
25	11,069.65	10,491.05	9,998.05	10,570.55	10,605.15							
26	11,069.65	10,582.60	10,130.65	10,617.80	10,605.15							
27	11,069.65	10,554.30	10,183.70	10,692.30	10,605.15							
28	11,069.65	10,492.85	10,121.25	10,692.30	10,688.65							
29	11,130.40		10,113.70	10,692.30	10,633.30							
30	11,049.65		10,113.70	10,739.35	10,614.35							
31	11,027.70		10,113.70		10,736.15							

The Standard Deviation of these values is 680.70.

We scale this value by the minimum recorded value in this period.

The minimum recorded value is 8,179.50.

So, the Scaled Standard Deviation is 8.32%. We will consider this as the Risk in Investment in Shares.

5.2 RETURN

Like the risks, we will calculate the returns from the instruments.

5.2.1 FIXED DEPOSIT

The returns gathered for the three banks are as follows.

Year	2018	2017	2016	2015	2014
HDFC Bank Ltd	7.10%	6.80%	6.50%	7.00%	7.90%
Ananda Cooperative Bank	8.50%	9.00%	9.00%	9.50%	10.00%
Gnana Shale Souharda Cooperative Bank	11.50%	13.00%	13.00%	13.50%	14.50%

We will take the average of the current Interest Rate as the Returns from Investment in Fixed Deposits.

Average of Current Returns = (7.10%+8.50%+11.50%)/3 = 9.03%

So, we will target 10% returns from Investment in Fixed Deposits.

5.2.2 MUTUAL FUND

To figure out the Risk and Return from Mutual Funds, I consulted three Investment Bankers. They are:-

1. Mr. S (C1)

2. Mr. R (C2)

3. Mr. D (C3)

The names and the companies of the consultants have been obfuscated.

From them, I got the following figures regarding the possible returns from Mutual Funds.

Consultant	OPTIMISTIC RETURNS		PESSIMISTIC RETURNS	
	Probability	Return	Probability	Return
C1	70%	20%	30%	5%
C2	60%	22%	40%	5%
C3	60%	18%	40%	8%

From these figures, we can calculate the Returns as predicted by each of the Consultants.

Consultant	Calculation for Return	Return
C1	70% * 20% + 30% * 5%	15.50%
C2	60% * 22% + 40% * 5%	15.20%
C3	60% * 18% + 40% * 8%	14.00%
	AVERAGE RETURN PREDICTED	**14.90%**

So, we will target <u>15%</u> returns from Investment in Mutual Funds.

5.2.3 SHARES

To figure out the Risk and Return from Shares, I consulted three Investment Bankers. They are:-

1. Mr. S (C1)

2. Mr. R (C2)

3. Mr. S (C3)

The names and the companies of the consultants have been obfuscated.

From them, I got the following figures regarding the possible returns from Shares.

	C1		C2		C3	
Probability	20%		30%		30%	
Returns		60%		50%		30%
Probability	70%		50%		40%	
Returns		20%		20%		15%
Probability	10%		20%		30%	
Returns		10%		-20%		-15%
Combined Return Formula	(20%*60%) + (70%*20%) + (10%*-10%)		(30%*50%) + (50%*20%) + (20%*-20%)		(30%*30%) + (40%*15) + (30%*-15%)	
Returns	25%		21%		10.5%	

Instead of taking the average in this case, I will take the prediction of Mr. S. This is because I have found that his advice has resulted in the best income from Shares for me.

So, we will consider returns from Investment in Shares as 25%.

5.3 CORRELATION BETWEEN ASSET CLASSES

Finding reliable data regarding the correlation between Investment in Fixed Deposits, Mutual Funds, and Shares is difficult. So, we will consider empirical values for the correlations based on economic intuitions.

It is noticed that Fixed Deposits and Mutual Funds could be more highly correlated. However, still, they are positively correlated. This is because when the Economy does well, generally, Fixed Deposit Rates fall as the REPO Rate is slashed, while returns from Mutual Funds boom. The opposite is the case when the Economy does better.

However, Fixed Deposits and Mutual Funds give positive returns in good times.

So, we will consider the correlation between Fixed Deposits and Mutual Funds to be 0.3.

We can argue a correlation between Fixed Deposits and Shares by the same intuition. **So, we will consider the correlation between Fixed Deposits and Shares as 0.1**. We consider a lower value here as Debt Instruments insulate Mutual Funds during a downturn in Equity Markets.

Mutual Funds and Shares generally move together. However, as Mutual Funds are also invested in Debt Instruments and Debt

Instruments move in the opposite direction to Equities, **we will consider the correlation between Mutual Funds and Shares to be 0.6**.

So, the correlation matrix is as follows:

	Fixed Deposit	Mutual Fund	Shares
Fixed Deposit	1.0		
Mutual Fund	0.3	1.0	
Shares	0.1	0.6	1.0

5.4 COEFFICIENT OF RISK AVERSION

There are three types of Investors. They are as follows.

1. **Risk Averse**: These Investors avoid taking Risk. The Coefficient of Risk Aversion for these Investors is >0.

2. **Risk Neutral**: These Investors are neutral to taking Risk. The Coefficient of Risk Aversion for these Investors is =0.

3. **Risk Seekers**: These Investors are willing to take Risk. The Coefficient of Risk Aversion for these Investors is <0.

Our Investor is an entrepreneur, and through Interview, we gather that our Investor is a Risk Seeker. Empirically, **we assign a value of -2 to our Investor's Coefficient of Risk Aversion**.

5.5 ALLOCATING FUNDS BETWEEN ASSET CLASSES

Now that we have all the building blocks, we allocate funds to the three Asset Classes by setting up a Linear Programming problem to maximize the Utility of the Investment for the Investor.

The initial state of the formulation looks as follows.

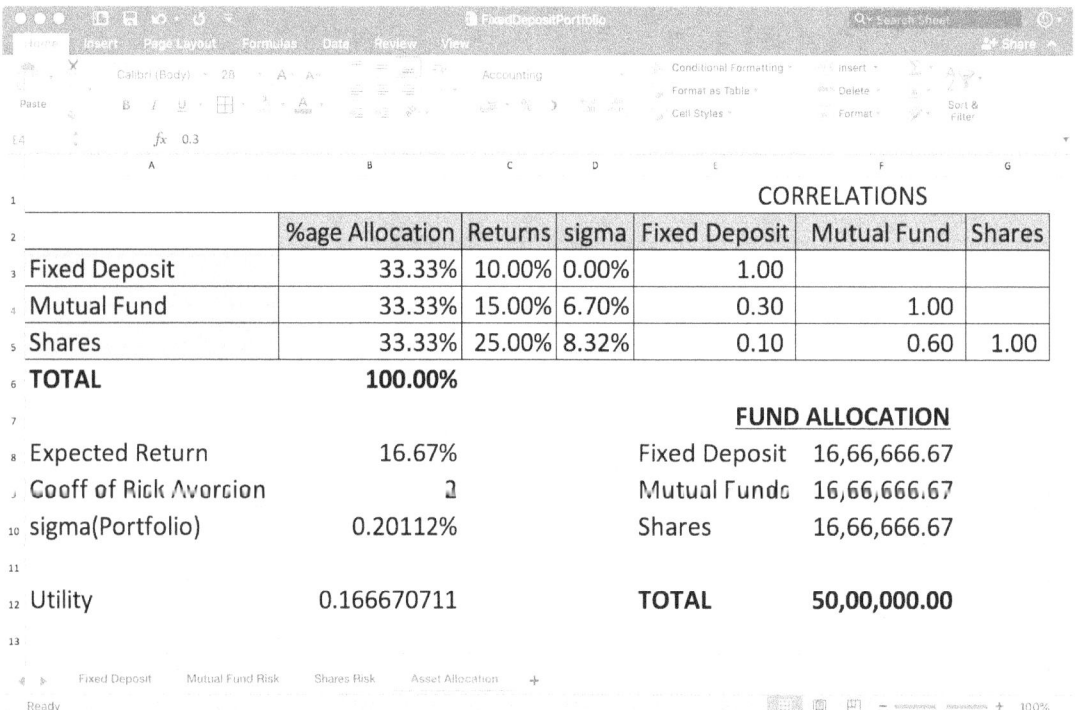

We start by allocating an equal amount of funds to each asset class.

The setup of the Linear Programming problem is as follows.

Set Objective: $B$12

To: ○ Max   Min   Value Of: [ ]

By Changing Variable Cells:

$B$3:$B$5

Subject to the Constraints:

$B$3 <= 0.4

$B$4 <= 0.4

$B$5 <= 0.4

$B$6 = 1

Add

Change

Delete

Reset All

Load/Save

☑ Make Unconstrained Variables Non-Negative

Select a Solving Method: GRG Nonlinear ▼   Options

Solving Method

Select the GRG Nonlinear engine for Solver Problems that are smooth nonlinear. Select the LP Simplex engine for linear Solver Problems, and select the Evolutionary engine for Solver problems that are non-smooth.

Close   Solve

Notice that we have planted the condition that the maximum allocation in an asset class can be 40%.

Now, we solve the Linear Programming problem to maximize the

Utility. The results are as follows.

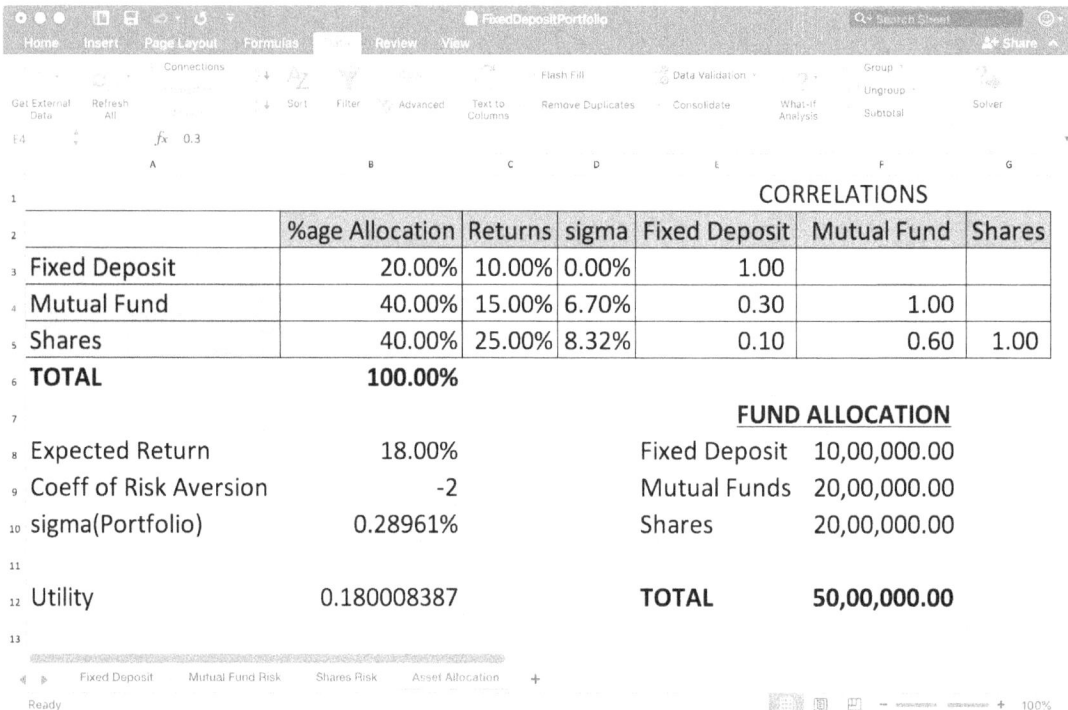

The optimum Fund Allocation is as follows.

Instrument	Allocated Amount (Rs.)
Fixed Deposits	Rs. 10,00,000.00
Mutual Funds	Rs. 20,00,000.00
Shares	Rs. 20,00,000.00

We notice that the **Expected Return is 18% from this portfolio**.

Also, **notice that the Risk from this Portfolio is almost**

eliminated.

6 APPLYING A MODEL FOR FUND ALLOCATION WITHIN EACH ASSET CLASS

Now that we have determined how much funds to allocate to each Asset Class, we select Assets within each Asset Class and allocate Funds to them.

6.1 FIXED DEPOSITS

We have already strategized regarding which Fixed Deposits to invest in. So, we need to allocate funds to each Fixed Deposit to minimize the Risk.

We set up the Linear Programming problem to minimize the risk. We start by allocating equal funds to the three Fixed Deposits. The initial setup is as follows.

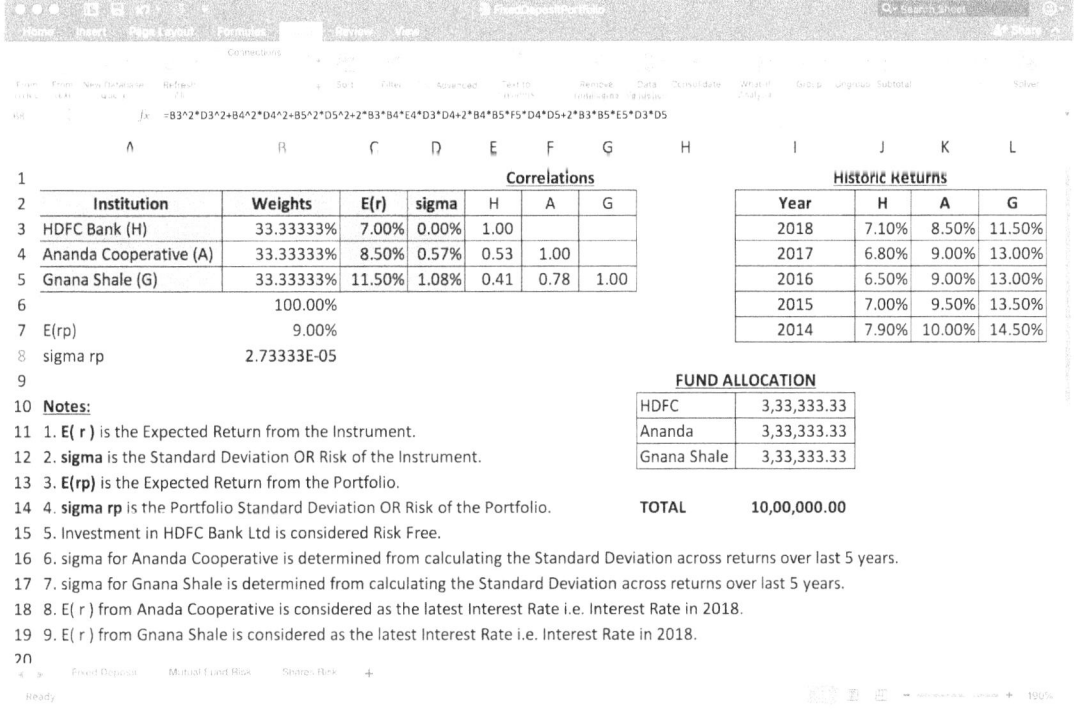

The Linear Programming Model set up in Excel is as follows.

Solver Parameters

Set Objective: $B$8

To: Max   ⦿ Min   Value Of: 0

By Changing Variable Cells:

$B$3:$B$5

Subject to the Constraints:

$B$3 >= 0.1	Add
$B$4 >= 0.1	
$B$5 >= 0.1	Change
$B$6 = 1	
$B$7 >= 0.1	Delete
	Reset All
	Load/Save

☐ Make Unconstrained Variables Non-Negative

Select a Solving Method: GRG Nonlinear ▼   Options

Solving Method

Select the GRG Nonlinear engine for Solver Problems that are smooth nonlinear. Select the LP Simplex engine for linear Solver Problems, and select the Evolutionary engine for Solver problems that are non-smooth.

Close   Solve

On solving for this Linear Programming Model, we get the following results.

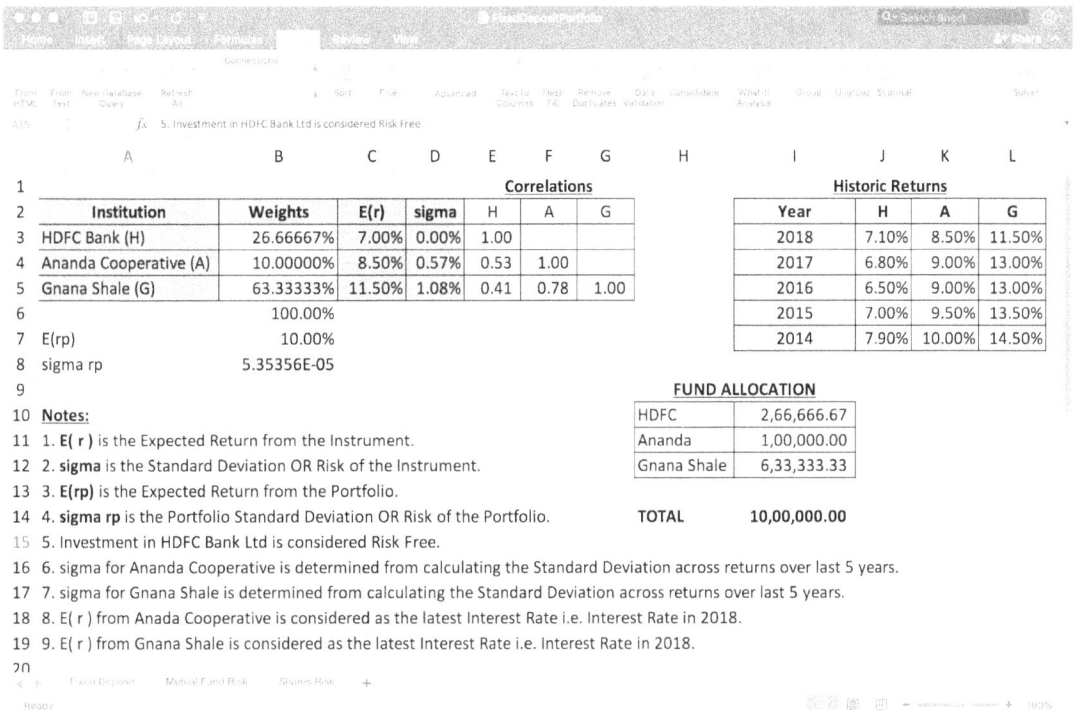

So, we make the final allocation as follows:

Institution	Amount Allocated
HDFC Bank Ltd	Rs. 2,60,000.00
Ananda Cooperative Bank	Rs. 1,10,000.00
Gnana Shale Souharda Cooperative Bank	Rs. 6,30,000.00

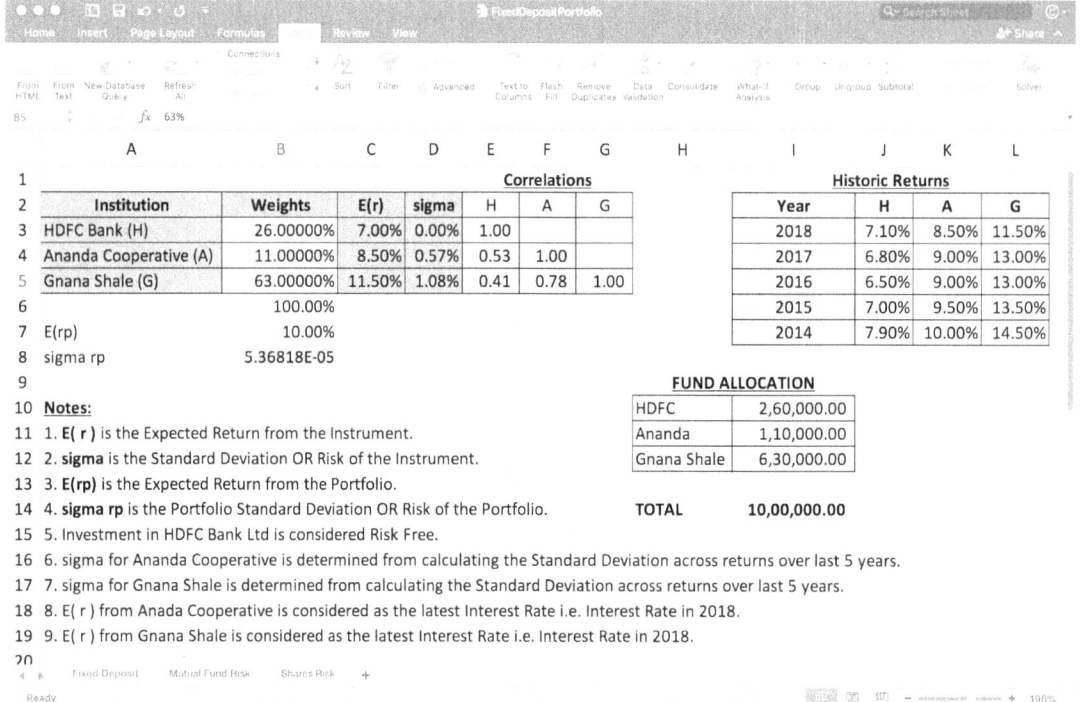

We notice that the Returns are still the same. However, Risk has increased, though it is negligible.

6.2 MUTUAL FUNDS

We first need to select the Mutual Funds to invest in. We must allocate funds once we have chosen the Mutual Funds to invest in.

6.2.1 SELECTING MUTUAL FUNDS

We must select two types of Mutual Funds – index-based Mutual Funds and Non-index-based Mutual Funds (i.e., Mutual Funds managed by Fund Managers).

6.2.1.1   SELECTING INDEX-BASED MUTUAL FUNDS

We will study the following four index-based Mutual Funds.

1. Franklin India Index Fund NSE NIFTY

2. HDFC Index Fund – NIFTY Plan

3. ICICI Prudential NIFTY Index Fund

4. SBI NIFTY Index Fund

The data gathered from www.economictimes.com are as follows.

FUND	RETURNS		
	1 year	**3 years**	**5 years**
Franklin India Index Fund	12.87%	10.52%	13.31%
HDFC Index Fund	14.21%	11.38%	14.16%
ICICI Prudential Index Fund	13.19%	10.83%	13.90%
SBI Index Fund	13.58%	10.89%	13.20%

Now, we calculate the Expected Returns (E_r), Standard Deviation

(σ) and the Sharpe Ratio.

FUND	E_r	σ	Sharpe Ratio
Franklin India Index Fund	12.23%	1.50%	3.42220
HDFC Index Fund	**13.25%**	**1.62%**	**3.79709**
ICICI Prudential Index Fund	12.84%	1.61%	3.44608
SBI Index Fund	12.56%	1.46%	3.74816

So, we select <u>HDFC Index Fund – NIFTY Plan</u>.

6.2.1.2   SELECTING DEBT-BASED MUTUAL FUNDS

We will study the following three Debt-based Mutual Funds. These

three are recommended by www.moneycontrol.com.

1. IDFC Bond Fund

2. Reliance Income Fund

3. SBU Dynamic Bond Fund

The data gathered from www.economictimes.com are as follows.

FUND	RETURNS		
	1 year	3 years	5 years
IDFC Bond Fund	8.73%	7.77%	7.77%
Reliance Income Fund	6.95%	8.59%	8.59%
SBI Dynamic Bond Fund	8.82%	8.89%	8.89%

Now, we calculate the Expected Returns (E_r), Standard Deviation

(σ) and the Sharpe Ratio.

FUND	E_r	σ	Sharpe Ratio
IDFC Bond Fund	8.09%	0.55%	1.78618
Reliance Income Fund	8.04%	0.95%	0.99628
SBI Dynamic Bond Fund	**8.87%**	**0.04%**	**43.71366**

So, we select SBI Dynamic Bond Fund.

6.2.1.3 SELECTING EQUITY-BASED MUTUAL FUNDS

We will study the following six Equity based Mutual Funds. These six are recommended by Axis Securities.

1. Axis Focused 25 Fund

2. Axis Long Term Equity Fund

3. Aditya Birla SL Frontline Equity Fund

4. Franklin India Bluechip Fund

5. IDFC Core Equity Fund

6. Reliance Small Cap Fund

6.2.1.3.1   AXIS FOCUSED 25 FUND

The allocation of funds is as follows:

Equity	91.24%	Rs. 1422.13 crores
Debt	9.21%	Rs. 342.07 crores
Others	-0.45%	– Rs. 16.71 crores

So, this is an Equity-Based Fund.

The portfolio of this fund is as follows.

Company	%age Allocation	Value (in Rs. Crores)	β
Kotak Mahindra Bank Ltd	7.85%	291.55	0.76
HDFC Bank Ltd	7.59%	281.74	0.69
Tata Consultancy Services Ltd	6.70%	248.95	0.25
Maruti Suzuki India Ltd	5.90%	219.20	0.92
Supreme Industries Ltd	5.88%	218.31	0.70
Shree Cement Ltd	5.58%	207.31	0.91
Bajaj Finance Ltd	5.01%	186.04	1.29
Bajaj Finserv Ltd	4.87%	180.93	1.33
Gruh Finance Ltd	4.36%	162.09	0.73
Motherson Sumi Systems Ltd	3.68%	136.79	1.29

We separate the Growth Stocks from the Value Stocks. For this, we find the **Price-to-Book Value (P/B)**. A low P/B is regarded as a Value Stock (V), and a high P/B is regarded as a Growth Stock (G).

Company	Book Value / Share	Price Per Share	Price-to-Book Value	G/V
Gruh Finance Ltd	37.76	681.80	18.06	G
Bajaj Finance Ltd	174.59	2,100.60	12.03	G

Supreme Industries Ltd	133.49	1,264.80	9.47	G
Shree Cement Ltd	2,209.71	16,102.00	7.29	G
Maruti Suzuki India Ltd	1,227.84	8,810.40	7.18	G
Kotak Mahindra Bank Ltd	211.66	1,304.70	6.16	G
Bajaj Finserv Ltd	1,014.90	5,770.95	5.69	G
HDFC Bank Ltd	423.71	2,063.60	4.87	G
Motherson Sumi Systems Ltd	74.85	307.65	4.11	G
Tata Consultancy Services Ltd	446.80	1,721.60	3.85	G

For all the Growth Stocks, we need to find the G-Score. And for all the Value Stocks, we need to find the F-Score.

Given here are the G-Score Calculations for the ten companies.

Company	G1	G2	G3	G4	G5	G6	G7	G8	G-Score	Weight	Contribution
Kotak Mahindra Bank Ltd	1	1	0	1	1	0	1	1	6	5.88%	0.4710
Tata Consultancy Services Ltd	1	1	1	1	1	1	1	0	7	7.59%	0.4690
HDFC Bank Ltd	1	1	0	1	1	0	1	1	6	5.01%	0.4554
Maruti Suzuki India Ltd	1	1	0	1	1	1	1	1	7	7.85%	0.4130
Shree Cement Ltd	1	1	0	1	1	1	1	0	6	5.90%	0.3348
Bajaj Finance Ltd	1	1	1	1	1	0	0	1	6	6.70%	0.3006
Supreme Industries Ltd	1	1	0	1	1	0	1	0	5	4.36%	0.2940
Bajaj Finserv Ltd	1	1	1	1	1	0	0	1	6	5.58%	0.2922
Motherson Sumi Systems Ltd	1	1	0	1	1	1	1	0	6	4.87%	0.2208
Gruh Finance Ltd	1	1	0	1	1	0	0	0	4	3.68%	0.1744
NET G-SCORE											3.4252

There are no Value Stocks and thus we do not calculate the F-Score.

So, the total score of this Fund is **3.4252**.

6.2.1.3.2 AXIS LONG TERM EQUITY FUND

The allocation of funds is as follows:

Equity	95.20%	Rs. 16703.95 crores
Debt	2.87%	Rs. 504.11 crores
Others	1.93%	Rs. 338.64 crores

So, this is an Equity-Based Fund.

The portfolio of this fund is as follows.

Company	%age Allocation	Value (in Rs. Crores)
HDFC Bank Ltd	7.78%	1,364.94
Tata Consultancy Services Ltd	7.65%	1,341.78
Kotak Mahindra Bank Ltd	7.62%	1,337.44
Pidilite Industries Ltd	6.41%	1,125.06
HDFC Ltd	6.05%	1,061.70
Bajaj Finance Ltd	5.22%	915.47
Gruh Finance Ltd	5.03%	883.09
Maruti Suzuki India Ltd	4.51%	791.70
Avenue Supermarts Ltd	4.33%	760.34
Motherson Sumi Systems Ltd	3.34%	586.45

We separate the Growth Stocks from the Value Stocks.

Company	Book Value / Share	Price Per Share	Price-to-Book Value	G/V
Avenue Supermarts Ltd	61.56	1,523.65	24.71	G
Gruh Finance Ltd	37.76	681.80	18.06	G
Pidilite Industries Ltd	70.18	1,078.05	15.33	G
Bajaj Finance Ltd	174.59	2,100.60	12.03	G
Maruti Suzuki India Ltd	1,227.84	8,810.40	7.18	G

Company					
Kotak Mahindra Bank Ltd	211.66	1,304.70	6.16	G
HDFC Bank Ltd	423.71	2,063.60	4.87	G
HDFC Ltd	399.58	1,823.55	4.57	G
Motherson Sumi Systems Ltd	74.85	307.65	4.11	G
Tata Consultancy Services Ltd	446.80	1,721.60	3.85	G

Given here are the G-Score Calculations for the ten companies.

Company	G1	G2	G3	G4	G5	G6	G7	G8	G-Score	Weight	Contribution
Tata Consultancy Services Ltd	1	1	1	1	1	1	1	0	7	7.65%	0.5355
HDFC Bank Ltd	1	1	0	1	1	0	1	1	6	7.78%	0.4668
Kotak Mahindra Bank Ltd	1	1	0	1	1	0	1	1	6	7.62%	0.4572
Pidilite Industries Ltd	1	1	0	1	1	1	0	1	6	6.41%	0.3846
HDFC Ltd	1	1	1	1	1	0	1	0	6	6.05%	0.3630
Maruti Suzuki India Ltd	1	1	0	1	1	1	1	1	7	4.51%	0.3157
Bajaj Finance Ltd	1	1	1	1	1	0	0	1	6	5.22%	0.3132
Avenue Supermarts Ltd	1	1	1	1	1	0	0	0	5	4.33%	0.2165
Gruh Finance Ltd	1	1	0	1	1	0	0	0	4	5.03%	0.2012
Motherson Sumi Systems Ltd	1	1	0	1	1	1	1	0	6	3.34%	0.2004
NET G-SCORE											3.4541

There are no Value Stocks and thus we do not calculate the F-Score.

So, the total score of this Fund is **3.4541**.

6.2.1.3.3   ADITYA BIRLA SL FRONTLINE EQUITY FUND

The allocation of funds is as follows:

Equity	96.98%	Rs. 19718.41 crores
Debt	2.34%	Rs. 476.69 crores
Others	0.67%	Rs. 136.50 crores

So, this is an Equity-Based Fund.

The portfolio of this fund is as follows.

Company	%age Allocation	Value (in Rs. Crores)
HDFC Bank Ltd	8.67%	1,762.54
ICICI Bank Ltd	5.09%	1,034.93
Infosys Ltd	4.84%	984.55
ITC Ltd	4.57%	929.22
Larsen & Toubro Ltd	2.80%	569.54
Maruti Suzuki India Ltd	2.76%	560.99
Yes Bank Ltd	2.38%	484.97
Mahindra & Mahindra Ltd	2.32%	470.84
HCL Technologies Ltd	2.15%	437.60
HDFC Ltd	2.12%	431.87

We separate the Growth Stocks from the Value Stocks.

Company	Book Value / Share	Price Per Share	Price-to-Book Value	G/V
Maruti Suzuki India Ltd	1,227.84	8,810.40	7.18	G
ITC Ltd	38.45	264.55	6.87	G
HDFC Bank Ltd	423.71	2,063.60	4.87	G
HDFC Ltd	399.58	1,823.55	4.57	G
Infosys Ltd	298.73	1,267.40	4.24	G
HCL Technologies Ltd	232.15	933.20	4.03	G
Yes Bank Ltd	111.82	331.65	2.97	G
Larsen & Toubro Ltd	576.44	1,323.20	2.30	V
ICICI Bank Ltd	187.98	293.00	1.56	V
Mahindra & Mahindra Ltd	634.07	913.90	1.44	V

Given here are the G-Score Calculations for the seven companies.

Company	G1	G2	G3	G4	G5	G6	G7	G8	G-Score	Weight	Contribution
HDFC Bank Ltd	1	1	0	1	1	0	1	1	6	8.67%	0.5202
ITC Ltd	1	1	1	1	1	1	1	0	7	4.57%	0.3199
Infosys Ltd	1	0	0	1	0	1	1	0	4	4.84%	0.1936
Maruti Suzuki India Ltd	1	1	0	1	1	1	1	1	7	2.76%	0.1932
HDFC Ltd	1	1	1	1	1	0	1	0	6	2.12%	0.1272
Yes Bank Ltd	1	0	0	1	1	0	0	1	4	2.38%	0.0952
HCL Technologies Ltd	1	0	0	1	1	0	0	0	3	2.15%	0.0645
NET G-SCORE										72.92%	1.5138

Given here are the F-Score Calculations for the three companies.

Company	F1	F2	F3	F4	F5	F6	F7	F8	F9	F-Score	Weight	Contribution
ICICI Bank Ltd	1	1	1	1	1	0	1	0	1	7	5.09%	0.3563
Larsen & Toubro Ltd	1	1	0	1	1	0	0	1	0	5	2.80%	0.1400
Mahindra & Mahindra Ltd	1	1	0	1	1	1	1	0	0	6	2.32%	0.1392
NET F-SCORE											27.08%	0.6355

So, the total score of this Fund is $((1.5138/7*10) * 72.92\% + (0.6355/3*10) * 27.08\%) =$ **2.1506**.

6.2.1.3.4 FRANKLIN INDIA BLUECHIP FUND

The allocation of funds is as follows:

Equity	96.68%	Rs. 7830.06 crores
Debt	0.00%	Rs. 0.00 crores
Others	3.32%	Rs. 268.87 crores

So, this is an Equity-Based Fund.

The portfolio of this fund is as follows.

Company	%age Allocation	Value (in Rs. Crores)
HDFC Bank Ltd	10.30%	834.39
Infosys Ltd	6.08%	492.72
Larsen & Toubro Ltd	4.87%	394.68
Bharti Airtel Ltd	4.52%	366.13
Yes Bank Ltd	4.27%	346.20
Mahindra & Mahindra Ltd	4.22%	341.49
ICICI Bank Ltd	3.71%	300.09
Axis Bank Ltd	3.37%	272.95
Kotak Mahindra Bank Ltd	3.30%	266.92
State Bank of India Ltd	2.60%	210.25

We separate the Growth Stocks from the Value Stocks.

Company	Book Value / Share	Price Per Share	Price-to-Book Value	G/V
Kotak Mahindra Bank Ltd	211.66	1,304.70	6.16	G
HDFC Bank Ltd	423.71	2,063.60	4.87	G
Infosys Ltd	290.73	1,267.10	4.24	G
Yes Bank Ltd	111.82	331.65	2.97	G
Larsen & Toubro Ltd	576.44	1,323.20	2.30	V
Axis Bank Ltd	250.44	522.55	2.08	V
Bharti Airtel Ltd	185.95	370.90	2.00	V
ICICI Bank Ltd	187.98	293.00	1.56	V
Mahindra & Mahindra Ltd	634.07	913.90	1.44	V
State Bank of India Ltd	263.25	276.85	1.05	V

Given here are the G-Score Calculations for the four companies.

Company	G1	G2	G3	G4	G5	G6	G7	G8	G-Score	Weight	Contribution
HDFC Bank Ltd	1	1	0	1	1	0	1	1	6	10.30%	0.6180
Infosys Ltd	1	0	0	1	0	1	1	0	4	6.08%	0.2432
Kotak Mahindra Bank Ltd	1	1	0	1	1	0	1	1	6	3.30%	0.1980
Yes Bank Ltd	1	0	0	1	1	0	0	1	4	4.27%	0.1708
NET G-SCORE										50.70%	1.2300

Given here are the F-Score Calculations for the six companies.

Company	F1	F2	F3	F4	F5	F6	F7	F8	F9	F-Score	Weight	Contribution
ICICI Bank Ltd	1	1	1	1	1	0	1	0	1	7	3.71%	0.2597
Mahindra & Mahindra Ltd	1	1	0	1	1	1	1	0	0	6	4.22%	0.2532
Larsen & Toubro Ltd	1	1	0	1	1	0	0	1	0	5	4.87%	0.2435
Bharti Airtel Ltd	1	0	1	0	1	0	1	0	1	5	4.52%	0.2260
Axis Bank Ltd	1	0	0	0	1	0	0	1	0	3	3.37%	0.1011
State Bank of India Ltd	1	0	0	0	1	0	1	0	0	3	2.60%	0.0780
NET F-SCORE											49.30%	1.1615

So, the total score of this Fund is ((1.23/4*10) * 50.7% +

(1.1615/6*10) * 49.3%) = **2.5134**.

6.2.1.3.5 IDFC CORE EQUITY FUND

The allocation of funds is as follows:

Equity	94.01%	Rs. 2611.71 crores
Debt	7.56%	Rs. 210.13 crores
Others	-1.58%	- Rs. 43.81 crores

So, this is an Equity-Based Fund.

The portfolio of this fund is as follows.

Company	%age Allocation	Value (in Rs. Crores)
HDFC Bank Ltd	6.91%	192.00
Infosys Ltd	4.17%	115.82
Larsen & Toubro Ltd	2.84%	78.90
Kotak Mahindra Bank Ltd	2.43%	67.57
ITC Ltd	2.14%	59.35
HDFC Ltd	2.12%	58.84
MRF Ltd	2.05%	56.84
Reliance Industries Ltd	2.01%	55.87
Mahindra & Mahindra Ltd	2.00%	55.50
Jindal Steel & Power Ltd	1.98%	55.06

We separate the Growth Stocks from the Value Stocks.

Company	Book Value / Share	Price Per Share	Price-to-Book Value	G/V
ITC Ltd	38.45	264.55	6.87	G
Kotak Mahindra Bank Ltd	211.66	1,304.70	6.16	G
HDFC Bank Ltd	423.71	2,063.60	4.87	G
HDFC Ltd	399.58	1,823.55	4.57	G
Infosys Ltd	298.73	1,267.40	4.24	G
MRF Ltd	20,373.94	74,359.80	3.65	G
Larsen & Toubro Ltd	576.44	1,323.20	2.30	V
Reliance Industries Ltd	501.59	1,015.55	2.02	V
Mahindra & Mahindra Ltd	634.07	913.90	1.44	V
Jindal Steel & Power Ltd	335.48	229.55	0.69	V

Given here are the G-Score Calculations for the six companies.

Company	G1	G2	G3	G4	G5	G6	G7	G8	G-Score	Weight	Contribution
HDFC Bank Ltd	1	1	0	1	1	0	1	1	6	6.91%	0.4146
Infosys Ltd	1	0	0	1	0	1	1	0	4	4.17%	0.1668
Kotak Mahindra Bank Ltd	1	1	0	1	1	0	1	1	6	2.43%	0.1458
ITC Ltd	1	1	1	1	1	1	1	0	7	2.14%	0.1498
HDFC Ltd	1	1	1	1	1	0	1	0	6	2.12%	0.1272
MRF Ltd	1	1	1	1	1	1	1	1	8	2.05%	0.1640
NET G-SCORE										69.18%	1.1682

Given here are the F-Score Calculations for the four companies.

Company	F1	F2	F3	F4	F5	F6	F7	F8	F9	F-Score	Weight	Contribution
Reliance Industries Ltd	1	1	1	1	1	1	1	1	1	9	2.01%	0.1809
Larsen & Toubro Ltd	1	1	0	1	1	0	0	1	0	5	2.84%	0.1420
Mahindra & Mahindra Ltd	1	1	0	1	1	1	1	0	0	6	2.00%	0.1200
Jindal Steel & Power Ltd	1	0	0	0	1	0	0	1	0	3	1.98%	0.0594
NET F-SCORE											30.82%	0.5023

So, the total score of this Fund is ((1.1682/6*10) * 69.18% + (0.5023/4*10) * 30.82%) = **1.7340**.

6.2.1.3.6   RELIANCE SMALL CAP FUND

The allocation of funds is as follows:

Equity	93.66%	Rs. 6503.81 crores
Debt	6.29%	Rs. 436.79 crores
Others	0.05%	Rs. 3.47 crores

So, this is an Equity-Based Fund.

The portfolio of this fund is as follows.

Company	%age Allocation	Value (in Rs. Crores)
HDFC Ltd	2.72%	188.92
VIP Industries Ltd	2.27%	157.61
Navin Fluorine International Ltd	2.26%	156.76
Deepak Nitrite Ltd	2.17%	150.65
Cyient Ltd	2.14%	148.41
Zydus Wellness Ltd	2.04%	141.65
LG Balakrishna & Bros Ltd	1.97%	136.61
RBL Bank Ltd	1.81%	125.91
Magma Fincorp Ltd	1.76%	122.15
Tejas Networks Ltd	1.70%	118.22

We separate the Growth Stocks from the Value Stocks.

Company	Book Value / Share	Price Per Share	Price-to-Book Value	G/V
Tejas Networks Ltd	6.76	312.15	46.57	G
VIP Industries Ltd	28.90	433.00	15.02	G
Zydus Wellness Ltd	145.31	1,447.10	9.99	G
RBL Bank Ltd	115.57	542.00	4.72	G
HDFC Ltd	399.58	1,823.55	4.57	G
Deepak Nitrite Ltd	54.86	244.55	4.47	G
Cyient Ltd	188.09	716.25	3.83	G
LG Balakrishna & Bros Ltd	306.67	612.05	2.01	V
Magma Fincorp Ltd	91.67	164.40	1.80	V
Navin Fluorine International Ltd	780.81	678.35	0.87	V

Given here are the G-Score Calculations for the seven companies.

Company	G1	G2	G3	G4	G5	G6	G7	G8	G-Score	Weight	Contribution
HDFC Ltd	1	1	1	1	1	0	1	0	6	2.72%	0.1632
VIP Industries Ltd	0	1	0	1	1	0	1	1	5	2.27%	0.1135
RBL Bank Ltd	1	1	0	1	1	0	0	1	5	1.81%	0.0905
Deepak Nitrite Ltd	1	0	0	1	1	1	0	0	4	2.17%	0.0868
Cyient Ltd	0	1	0	1	1	1	0	0	4	2.14%	0.0856
Tejas Networks Ltd	1	1	1	1	0	0	1	0	5	1.70%	0.0850
Zydus Wellness Ltd	1	1	0	1	1	0	0	0	4	2.04%	0.0816
NET G-SCORE										71.26%	0.7062

Given here are the F-Score Calculations for the three companies.

Company	F1	F2	F3	F4	F5	F6	F7	F8	F9	F-Score	Weight	Contribution
Navin Fluorine Intl Ltd	1	1	0	1	1	1	1	0	0	6	2.26%	0.1356
LG Balakrishna & Bros Ltd	0	1	0	1	1	0	0	1	1	5	1.97%	0.0985
Magma Fincorp Ltd	1	1	0	1	1	0	0	1	0	5	1.76%	0.0880
NET F-SCORE											28.74%	0.3221

So, the total score of this Fund is ((0.7062/7*10) * 71.26% + (0.3221/3*10) * 28.74%) = **1.0275**.

6.2.1.3.7   FINAL SELECTION OF EQUITY-BASED MUTUAL FUNDS

Based on our analysis, we find that the scores of the six Mutual Funds are as follows.

FUND	SCORE
Axis Long Term Equity Fund	**3.4541**
Axis Focused 25 Fund	3.4252
Franklin India Bluechip Fund	**2.5134**
Aditya Birla SL Frontline Equity Fund	**2.1506**
IDFC Core Equity Fund	1.7340
Reliance Small Cap Fund	1.0275

In our list and according to our analysis, the top two funds are from Axis Mutual Funds. So, we will select one of them for diversification between Fund Managers. So, **we choose Axis Long Term Equity Fund, Franklin India Bluechip Fund and Aditya Birla SL Frontline Equity Fund**.

6.2.2 ALLOCATING FUNDS TO MUTUAL FUNDS

We allocate funds to the selected Mutual Funds such that the Treynor Ratio of the portfolio of Mutual Funds is maximized. So, allocate equal amounts to each Mutual Fund and solve the Linear Programming Problem.

The initial setup is as follows.

FUND	Weight	β	E(r)	σ	Allocation
			Risk Free Rate --->		7.10%
			TOTAL FUNDS --->		20,00,000.00
HDFC Index Fund NIFTY Plan	20.00%	0.99	9.89%	13.51%	4,00,000.00
SBI Dynamic Bond Fund	20.00%	1.58	7.23%	4.04%	4,00,000.00
Axis Long Term Equity Fund	20.00%	0.82	12.52%	12.46%	4,00,000.00
Franklin India Bluechip Fund	20.00%	0.93	8.36%	12.86%	4,00,000.00
Aditya Birla SL frontline Equity Fund	20.00%	0.93	10.33%	13.08%	4,00,000.00
	100.00%				
Portfolio Beta		1.05			
Expected Return from Portfolio			9.67%		
Portfolio Risk (Sigma)				8.02%	
Sharpe Ratio	0.32				
Treynor Ratio	0.02				

The LPP Setup is as follows.

Set Objective: $B$16

To: ● Max   ○ Min   Value Of: [0]

By Changing Variable Cells:

$B$4:$B$8

Subject to the Constraints:

$B$4 <= .25	Add
$B$4 >= .08	
$B$5 <= .25	Change
$B$5 >= .08	
$B$6 <= .25	Delete
$B$6 >= .08	
$B$7 <= .25	
$B$7 >= .08	Reset All
$B$8 <= .25	
$B$8 >= .08	Load/Save
$B$9 = 1	

☑ Make Unconstrained Variables Non-Negative

Select a Solving Method: GRG Nonlinear ▼   Options

Solving Method

Select the GRG Nonlinear engine for Solver Problems that are smooth nonlinear. Select the LP Simplex engine for linear Solver Problems, and select the Evolutionary engine for Solver problems that are non-smooth.

Close   Solve

The Final allocation of Funds is as follows.

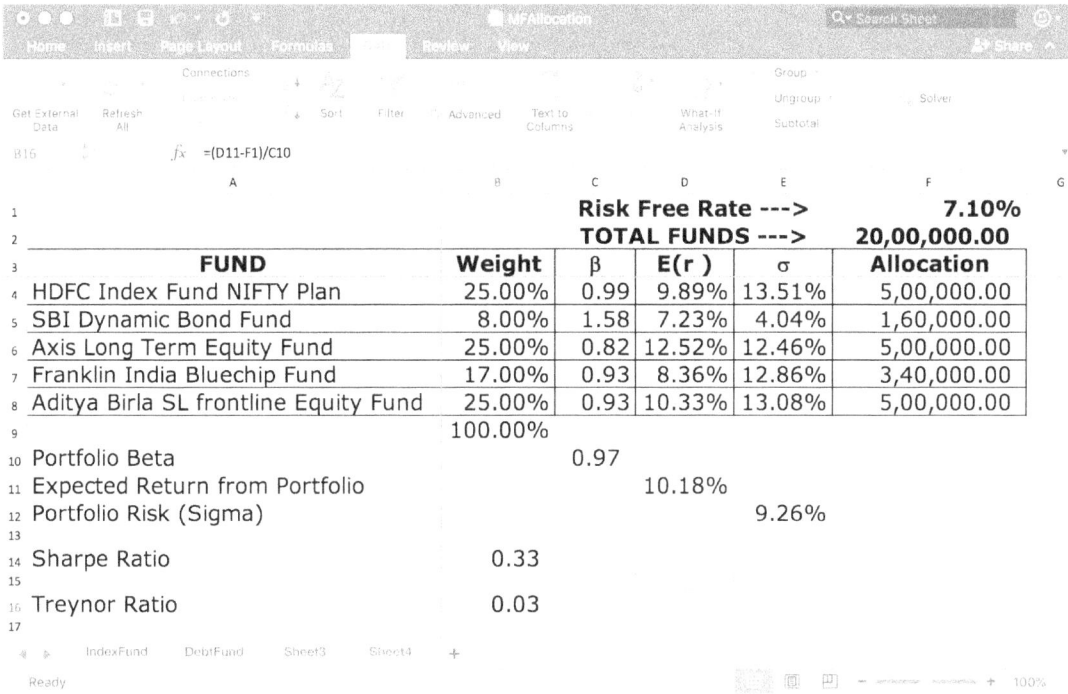

So, our allocation of funds in Mutual Funds is as follows.

MUTUAL FUND	Allocation
HDFC Index Fund NIFTY Plan	Rs. 5,00,000
SBI Dynamic Bond Fund	Rs. 1,60,000
Axis Long Term Equity Fund	Rs. 5,00,000
Franklin India Bluechip Fund	Rs. 3,40,000
Aditya Birla SL Frontline Equity Fund	Rs. 5,00,000

6.3 SHARES

We first need to select the Shares to invest in. Once we have chosen the Shares to invest in, we must allocate funds.

6.3.1 SELECTING SHARES

We need to select Shares based on three different strategies. We make the selection through the strategies below.

6.3.1.1   SELECTING SHARES BASED ON SUE SCORE

SUE is the acronym for **Standardized Unexpected Earning**.

$$\textbf{SUE Score} = {}^{\textbf{(Actual EPS – Expected EPS)}} / {}_{\textbf{(Standard Deviation of EPS)}}$$

- ☐ **EPS** stands for Earning Per Share.

- ☐ **Actual EPS** is the current EPS released in the last year's Financial Statements.

- ☐ **Expected EPS** is calculated by finding the Average of the EPS at the end of the last four years (before the current year).

- ☐ **Standard Deviation of EPS** is calculated by finding the Standard Deviation of the last four year's EPS.

After finding the SUE Score of the Stocks of interest, order them in the descending order of the SUE Score.

As a thumb rule, we must sell all Stocks with a negative SUE Score.

Also, we must consider selling all Stocks with a very low SUE Score.

73

We must consider buying the Stock with the highest SUE Scores (positive values only).

This strategy must be applied soon after the companies' annual results are announced. So, this is the ideal time to use this strategy.

In our case, we are building a new portfolio. So, we will only take the case where **we buy the Shares with a high SUE Score**.

I have collected the EPS for different companies and arranged them by SUE Score. The data can be seen in the table below.

Stock	2014	2015	2016	2017	Expected EPS	Standard Deviation	Actual EPS	SUE
DLF Ltd	3.63	3.03	1.72	4.01	3.10	1.0030	25.02	21.8560
Titan Company Ltd	8.28	9.19	7.60	8.01	8.27	0.6740	12.73	6.6168
HDFC Ltd	50.93	55.65	64.50	69.56	60.16	8.4208	96.77	4.3476
Hindustan Unilever Ltd	18.24	20.17	19.22	20.79	19.61	1.1158	24.09	4.0196
Chambal Fertilisers and Chemicals Ltd	5.73	5.90	7.12	5.31	6.02	0.7773	8.70	3.4543
ITC Ltd	7.45	8.04	7.74	8.47	7.93	0.4359	9.24	3.0166
JSW Steel Ltd	1.75	7.32	(1.40)	14.66	5.58	7.0442	25.71	2.8573
Kotak Mahindra Bank Ltd	16.00	19.72	18.86	26.84	20.36	4.6065	32.54	2.6452
Bharat Electronics Ltd	3.45	3.60	4.53	5.07	4.16	0.7709	6.20	2.6432
Infosys Ltd	46.57	54.07	58.96	62.73	55.58	6.9763	73.66	2.5913
Tata Elxsi Ltd	12.06	16.52	24.86	27.83	20.32	7.2956	38.54	2.4977
HDFC Bank Ltd	36.45	42.64	50.63	59.63	47.34	10.0424	71.28	2.3841
Capital First Ltd	7.19	12.56	18.21	24.52	15.62	7.4464	33.09	2.3461
Yes Bank Ltd	6.94	9.56	12.03	14.63	10.79	3.2974	18.38	2.3018
Reliance Industries Ltd	38.25	40.04	50.45	50.53	44.82	6.5908	56.94	1.8393
Jain Irrigation Systems Ltd	(0.86)	1.20	1.02	3.53	1.22	1.7984	4.42	1.7780

Minda Corporation Ltd	3.92	4.32	5.16	4.62	4.51	0.5224	5.37	1.6558
LIC Housing Finance Ltd	26.12	27.65	33.05	38.49	31.33	5.6247	39.91	1.5259
Just Dial Ltd	17.19	19.70	20.55	17.45	18.72	1.6596	21.25	1.5229
HCL Technologies Ltd	46.50	52.04	39.72	60.32	49.65	8.7195	62.63	1.4892
Maruti Suzuki India Ltd	94.47	126.07	181.99	248.67	162.80	67.7249	260.86	1.4479
MindTree Ltd	27.03	32.04	32.93	24.92	29.23	3.8731	34.78	1.4330
Dabur India Ltd	5.24	6.07	7.11	7.25	6.42	0.9451	7.69	1.3464
Tata Consultancy Services Ltd	97.69	101.35	123.20	133.45	113.92	17.2139	135.21	1.2366
Vedanta Ltd	21.24	(52.77)	(41.38)	14.83	(14.52)	37.9681	27.82	1.1151
Hindustan Petroleum Corp Ltd	7.09	9.83	30.68	54.05	25.41	21.8051	47.37	1.0070
Castrol India Ltd	4.80	6.22	6.78	6.99	6.20	0.9867	7.02	0.8336
Suzlon Energy Ltd	(14.16)	(24.70)	1.16	1.71	(9.00)	12.7938	1.26	0.8018
Kiri Industries Ltd	5.22	79.88	73.71	95.66	63.62	40.0138	93.46	0.7458
Bharat Forge Ltd	6.54	11.28	16.38	14.57	12.19	4.3194	15.13	0.6801
ACC Ltd	61.88	31.30	35.05	49.23	44.37	13.9989	51.32	0.4968
India Cements Ltd	(7.92)	0.00	3.00	4.02	0.20	5.8084	2.15	0.3357
Cummins India Ltd	16.70	27.85	26.02	26.56	24.28	5.1130	25.68	0.2733
Jet Airways Ltd	(363.54)	(184.63)	106.66	38.60	(100.73)	214.8889	(56.03)	0.2080
Federal Bank Ltd	4.97	6.17	2.83	5.03	4.75	1.3940	4.74	(0.0072)
Granules India Ltd	3.71	4.45	5.68	7.19	5.26	1.5231	5.22	(0.0246)
Bank of Baroda Ltd	22.81	23.29	17.69	(21.99)	10.45	21.7747	7.88	(0.1180)
Canara Bank Ltd	65.20	55.46	58.64	(46.70)	33.15	53.3876	22.74	(0.1950)
Siemens Ltd	16.94	32.99	81.85	31.93	40.93	28.2490	33.61	(0.2590)
Tata Motors Ltd	43.01	42.99	34.10	21.95	35.51	9.9676	31.13	(0.4397)
REC Ltd	24.01	27.06	28.82	31.97	27.97	3.3283	25.98	(0.5964)
Oil India Ltd	24.87	21.70	17.30	13.28	19.29	5.0670	16.04	(0.6409)
Sintex Industries Ltd	11.52	12.24	13.83	2.46	10.01	5.1267	2.39	(1.4868)
Biocon Ltd	6.90	8.29	9.17	10.20	8.64	1.3982	6.21	(1.7380)
Coal India Ltd	23.92	21.73	22.59	14.93	20.79	4.0108	13.60	(1.7933)
State Bank of India Ltd	18.99	22.76	15.75	0.30	14.45	9.8587	(5.11)	(1.9840)
Karnataka Bank Ltd	13.45	19.51	17.95	16.00	16.73	2.6146	11.52	(1.9917)

Dr. Reddy Laboratories Ltd	115.35	137.11	124.89	77.93	113.82	25.5304	57.06	(2.2232)
Bharti Airtel Ltd	7.55	11.56	15.20	9.51	10.96	3.2695	2.75	(2.5096)
Axis Bank Ltd	26.86	31.42	35.04	16.51	27.46	8.0291	1.78	(3.1980)
Apollo Tyres Ltd	19.94	19.21	22.06	21.59	20.70	1.3465	12.65	(5.9783)

So, we select the following Shares based on SUE Score.

1. DLF Ltd

2. Titan Company Ltd

3. HDFC Ltd

4. Hindustan Unilever Ltd

6.3.1.2   SELECTING SHARES BASED ON SLOAN SCORE

Based on recommendation from Investment Bankers, I have collected names of some Stocks to invest in. I investigate these Stocks based on their Sloan Score. These Stocks are as follows.

1. Tata Consultancy Services Ltd (TCS)

2. Reliance Industries Ltd

3. Siemens Ltd

4. Infosys Ltd

5. ITC Ltd

6. Karnataka Bank Ltd

7. LIC Housing Finance Ltd

8. National Aluminium Company Ltd (NALCO)

6.3.1.2.1 TATA CONSULTANCY SERVICES LTD (TCS)

From the Annual Report of TCS, we gather the following.

Account Head	(All figures are in crores of Rs.)	
	2016-17	2015-16
Cash and bank balances	1,316	4,806
TOTAL CURRENT ASSETS	68,619	53,377
TOTAL ASSETS	89,758	77,417
Current Liabilities	10,701	11,309
TOTAL SHORT-TERM DEBTS	200	113
Tax expense	6,413	6,264
Revenue from Operations	117,966	108,646
Depreciation and amortization expense	1,575	1,459

Based on these figures, we can calculate the components of the

Sloan Score.

ΔCurrent Assets = 68,619 – 53,377 = 15,242

ΔCash = 1,316 – 4,806 = -3,490

ΔCurrent Liabilities = 10,701 – 11,309 = -608

ΔTotal Short-Term Debts = 200 – 113 = 87

ΔTax Payable = 6,413 – 6,264 = 149

Accruals (**A**)	(15,242 – (-3,490)) – ((-608) – 87 – 149) – 1,575	18,001
Total Revenue from Continuous Operations (**I**)		117,966
A Normalized = A / (Average Assets of Last 2 Year)	18,001 / 83,587.50	0.215
I Normalized = I / (Average Assets of Last 2 Year)	117,966 / 83,587.50	1.411
Sloan Score	**1.411 – 0.215**	**1.196**

6.3.1.2.2 RELIANCE INDUSTRIES LTD (RIL)

From the Annual Report of RIL, we gather the following.

Account Head	(All figures are in crores of Rs.)	
	2016-17	2015-16
Cash and bank balances	323.58	241.26
TOTAL CURRENT ASSETS	4,388.24	11,558.64
TOTAL ASSETS	35,480.63	35,363.82
Current Liabilities	2,060.22	2,907.62
TOTAL SHORT-TERM DEBTS	0	0
Tax expense	661.15	817.52
Revenue from Operations	9,320.86	8,969.33
Depreciation and amortization expense	1,443.25	1,232.45

Based on these figures, we can calculate the components of the

Sloan Score.

ΔCurrent Assets = 4,388.24 – 11,558.64 = -7,170.40

ΔCash = 323.58 – 241.26 = 82.32

ΔCurrent Liabilities = 2,060.22 – 2,907.62 = -847.40

ΔTotal Short-Term Debts = 0 – 0 = 0

ΔTax Payable = 661.15 – 817.52 = -156.37

Accruals (**A**)	((-7,170.40) – 82.32) – ((-847.40) – 0 – (-156.37)) – 1,443.25	-8,004.94
Total Revenue from Continuous Operations (**I**)		117,966
A Normalized = A / (Average Assets of Last 2 Year)	(-8,004.94) / 35,422.225	-0.226
I Normalized = I / (Average Assets of Last 2 Year)	9,320.86 / 35,422.225	0.263
Sloan Score	**0.263 – (-0.226)**	**0.489**

6.3.1.2.3 SIEMENS LTD

From the Annual Report of Siemens, we gather the following.

Account Head	(All figures are in lakhs of Rs.)	
	2016-17	2015-16
Cash and bank balances	8,375	10,604
TOTAL CURRENT ASSETS	58,429	55,329
TOTAL ASSETS	1,33,804	1,25,717
Current Liabilities	43,394	42,916
TOTAL SHORT-TERM DEBTS	5,447	6,206
Tax expense	2,042	1,773
Revenue from Operations	83,049	79,644
Depreciation and amortization expense	3,211	2,764

Based on these figures, we can calculate the components of the Sloan Score.

ΔCurrent Assets = 58,429 – 55,329 = 3,100

ΔCash = 8,375 – 10,604 = -2,229

ΔCurrent Liabilities = 43,394 – 42,916 = 478

ΔTotal Short-Term Debts = 5,447 – 6,206 = -759

ΔTax Payable = 2,042 – 1,773 = 269

Accruals (**A**)	(3,100 – (-2,229)) – (478 – (-759) – 269) – 3,211	1,150
Total Revenue from Continuous Operations (**I**)		83,049
A Normalized = A / (Average Assets of Last 2 Year)	1,150 / 1,29,760.5	0.009
I Normalized = I / (Average Assets of Last 2 Year)	83,049 / 1,29,760.5	0.640
Sloan Score	**0.640 – 0.009**	**0.631**

6.3.1.2.4 INFOSYS LTD

From the Annual Report of Infosys, we gather the following.

Account Head	(All figures are in crores of Rs.)	
	2016-17	2015-16
Cash and bank balances	16,770	19,153
TOTAL CURRENT ASSETS	44,090	47,682
TOTAL ASSETS	75,877	79,885
Current Liabilities	11,662	11,786
TOTAL SHORT-TERM DEBTS	0	0
Tax expense	4,003	5,068
Revenue from Operations	61,941	59,289
Depreciation and amortization expense	1,863	1,703

Based on these figures, we can calculate the components of the

Sloan Score.

ΔCurrent Assets = 44,090 – 47,682 = -3,592

ΔCash = 16,770 – 19,153 = -2,383

ΔCurrent Liabilities = 11,662 – 11,786 = -124

ΔTotal Short-Term Debts = 0 – 0 = 0

ΔTax Payable = 4,003 – 5,068 = -1,065

Accruals (**A**)	((-3,592) – (-2,383)) – ((-124) – 0 – (-1,065)) – 1,863	-4,013
Total Revenue from Continuous Operations (**I**)		61,941
A Normalized = A / (Average Assets of Last 2 Year)	-4,013 / 77,881	-0.052
I Normalized = I / (Average Assets of Last 2 Year)	61,941 / 77,881	0.795
Sloan Score	**0.795 – (-0.052)**	**0.847**

6.3.1.2.5 ITC LTD

From the Annual Report of ITC, we gather the following.

Account Head	(All figures are in crores of Rs.)	
	2016-17	2015-16
Cash and bank balances	156.15	75.79
TOTAL CURRENT ASSETS	26,269.10	24,862.50
TOTAL ASSETS	55,943.27	51,691.88
Current Liabilities	9,238.39	8,499.89
TOTAL SHORT-TERM DEBTS	0.01	3.60
Tax expense	6,830.07	6,354.27
Revenue from Operations	55,448.46	51,944.57
Depreciation and amortization expense	1,152.79	1,077.40

Based on these figures, we can calculate the components of the

Sloan Score.

ΔCurrent Assets = 26,269.10 – 24,862.50 = 1,460.60

ΔCash = 156.15 – 75.79 = 80.36

ΔCurrent Liabilities = 9,238.39 – 8,499.89 = 738.50

ΔTotal Short-Term Debts = 0.01 – 3.60 = -3.59

ΔTax Payable = 6,830.07 – 6,354.27 = 475.80

Accruals (**A**)	(1,460.60 – 80.36) – (738.50 – (-3.59) – 475.80) – 1,152.79	-92.84
Total Revenue from Continuous Operations (**I**)		55,448.46
A Normalized = A / (Average Assets of Last 2 Year)	-92.84 / 53,817.575	-0.002
I Normalized = I / (Average Assets of Last 2 Year)	55,448.46 / 53,817.575	1.030
Sloan Score	**1.030 – (-0.002)**	**1.032**

6.3.1.2.6 KARNATAKA BANK LTD

From the Annual Report of Kar Bank, we gather the following.

Account Head	(All figures are in lakhs of Rs.)	
	2016-17	2015-16
Cash and bank balances	2,645.62	2,488.45
TOTAL CURRENT ASSETS	36,947.37	34,294.15
TOTAL ASSETS	56,500.33	51,836.60
Current Liabilities	2,321.53	2,438.93
TOTAL SHORT-TERM DEBTS	1,051.48	1,037.76
Tax expense	185.23	330.97
Revenue from Operations	4,992.21	4,698.42
Depreciation and amortization expense	242.14	203.33

Based on these figures, we can calculate the components of the Sloan Score.

ΔCurrent Assets = 36,947.37 − 34,294.15 = 2,653.22

ΔCash = 2,645.62 − 2,488.45 = 157.17

ΔCurrent Liabilities = 2,321.53 − 2,438.93 = -117.40

ΔTotal Short-Term Debts = 1,051.48 − 1,037.76 = 13.72

ΔTax Payable = 185.23 − 330.97 = -145.74

Accruals (**A**)	(2,653.22 − 157.17) − ((-117.40) − 13.72 − (-145.74)) − 242.14	2,239.29
Total Revenue from Continuous Operations (**I**)		4,992.21
A Normalized = A / (Average Assets of Last 2 Year)	2,239.29 / 54,168.465	0.041
I Normalized = I / (Average Assets of Last 2 Year)	4,992.21 / 54,168.465	0.092
Sloan Score	**0.092 − 0.041**	**0.051**

6.3.1.2.7   LIC HOUSING FINANCE LTD

From the Annual Report of LIC HFL, we gather the following.

Account Head	(All figures are in lakhs of Rs.)	
	2016-17	2015-16
Cash and bank balances	2,529.23	3,284.44
TOTAL CURRENT ASSETS	2,958.10	3,762.75
TOTAL ASSETS	4,574.13	4,857.26
Current Liabilities	848.26	1,201.66
TOTAL SHORT-TERM DEBTS	216.86	249.11
Tax expense	-79.96	13.00
Revenue from Operations	333.69	0.09
Depreciation and amortization expense	11.02	12.19

Based on these figures, we can calculate the components of the Sloan Score.

ΔCurrent Assets = 2,958.10 – 3,762.75 = -804.65

ΔCash = 2,529.23 – 3,284.44 = -755.21

ΔCurrent Liabilities = 848.26 – 1,201.66 = -353.40

ΔTotal Short-Term Debts = 216.86 – 249.11 = -32.25

ΔTax Payable = -79.96 – 13.00 = -92.96

Accruals (**A**)	((-804.65) – (-755.21)) – ((-353.40) – (-32.25) – (-92.96)) – 11.02	167.73
Total Revenue from Continuous Operations (**I**)		333.69
A Normalized = A / (Average Assets of Last 2 Year)	167.73 / 4,715.695	0.036
I Normalized = I / (Average Assets of Last 2 Year)	333.69 / 4,715.695	0.071
Sloan Score	**0.071 – 0.036**	**0.035**

6.3.1.2.8   NATIONAL ALUMINIUM COMPANY LTD

From the Annual Report of NALCO, we gather the following.

Account Head	(All figures are in crores of Rs.)	
	2016-17	2015-16
Cash and bank balances	2,287.23	5,103.15
TOTAL CURRENT ASSETS	5,655.79	7,343.65
TOTAL ASSETS	14,501.65	16,710.19
Current Liabilities	2,651.93	1,981.95
TOTAL SHORT-TERM DEBTS	0	0
Tax expense	219.52	366.93
Revenue from Operations	8,050.02	7,269.23
Depreciation and amortization expense	480.36	426.12

Based on these figures, we can calculate the components of the Sloan Score.

ΔCurrent Assets = 5,544.79– 7,343.65 = -1,687.86

ΔCash = 2,287.23 – 5,103.15 = -2,815.92

ΔCurrent Liabilities = 2,651.93 – 1,981.95 = 669.98

ΔTotal Short-Term Debts = 0 – 0 = 0

ΔTax Payable = 219.52 – 366.93 = -147.41

Accruals (**A**)	((-1,687.86) – (-2,815.92)) – (669.98 – 0 – (-147.41)) – 11.02	-169.69
Total Revenue from Continuous Operations (**I**)		8,050.02
A Normalized = A / (Average Assets of Last 2 Year)	-169.69 / 15,605.92	-0.011
I Normalized = I / (Average Assets of Last 2 Year)	8,050.02 / 15,605.92	0.516
Sloan Score	**0.516 – (-0.011)**	**0.527**

6.3.1.2.9 MAKING THE SELECTION

We arrange the companies by the Sloan Score in descending order.

Company	Sloan Score	Percentile
Tata Consultancy Services Ltd	1.196	100
ITC Ltd	1.032	88
Infosys Ltd	0.847	75
Siemens Ltd	0.631	63
National Aluminium Company Ltd	0.527	50
Reliance Industries Ltd	0.489	38
Karnataka Bank Ltd	0.051	25
LIC Housing Finance Ltd	0.035	13

So, we select the following Shares based on SLOAN Score.

1. Tata Consultancy Services Ltd

2. ITC Ltd

6.3.1.3 SELECTING SHARES BASED ON PAIR TRADING

With the Government working on providing Electricity to All, the Power Generating Companies are expected to do well in the coming years. So, for Pair Trading, we will try to select a Pair from the Power Generating Companies.

An allied industry to the Power Generation Industry is the Coal Industry. 37% of the fuel requirement of the Power Generating Companies is met by the Coal industry. So, when the Coal becomes costlier, Power Industry has adverse effect and the vice versa.

So, we will form a Pair between Power Generating Companies and the Coal Producing Companies.

6.3.1.3.1 FORMING PAIR FROM POWER GENERATING INDUSTRY

The Stocks being studied are as follows:

1. Gujarat Industries Power Company Ltd. (GIPCL)

2. Jaiprakash Power Ventures Ltd. (JPVL)

3. JSW Energy Ltd. (JSW)

4. NHPC Ltd. (NHPC)

5. NTPC Ltd. (NTPC)

6. Power Grid Corporation India Ltd. (PGRID)

7. Reliance Industries Ltd. (RIL)

8. SJVN Ltd. (SJVN)

The following steps were followed:

1. The Historical Prices from 1-Jun-2017 to 31-May-2018 were collected for each of the Stocks.

2. From the Historical Prices gathered in Step 1, the normalized prices of each day for each Stocks were calculated as (Stock Price – Mean(Stock Prices)) / Standard Deviation(Stock Prices).

3. From the normalized prices determined in Step 2, the distance was calculated for each day for each pair by squaring the difference between the normalized prices for the day of each pair.

4. Lastly, the square of the distances determined in Step 3 were summed to find the distance between each pair. This figure is provided in the table below.

	GIPCL	JPVL	JSW	NHPC	NTPC	PGRID	RIL	SJVN
GIPCL								
JPVL	73.93							
JSW	373.48	252.88						
NHPC	379.05	450.83	607.67					
NTPC	270.75	230.36	199.22	620.60				
PGRID	367.39	495.96	780.77	402.08	474.66			
RIL	484.97	599.09	861.60	210.93	686.01	193.01		
SJVN	356.87	253.64	145.23	493.60	338.50	746.79	722.27	

The least distance is found between GIPCL and JPVL.

So, we form a pair between <u>Gujarat Industries Power Company Ltd</u> and <u>Jaiprakash Power Ventures Ltd</u>.

6.3.1.3.2 FORMING PAIR BETWEEN POWER GENERATING INDUSTRY AND COAL INDUSTRY

The Stocks from Power Industry being studied are as follows:

1. Gujarat Industries Power Company Ltd. (GIPCL)

2. Jaiprakash Power Ventures Ltd. (JPVL)

3. JSW Energy Ltd. (JSW)

4. NHPC Ltd. (NHPC)

5. NTPC Ltd. (NTPC)

6. Power Grid Corporation India Ltd. (PGRID)

7. Reliance Industries Ltd. (RIL)

8. SJVN Ltd. (SJVN)

The Stocks from Coal Industry being studied are as follows:

1. Coal India Ltd (CIL)

2. Gujarat Mineral Development Corporation Ltd (GMDC)

3. Gujarat Natural Resources Ltd (GNRL)

4. Auroma Coke Ltd (ACL)

5. Austral Coke & Projects Ltd (ACPL)

The following steps were followed:

1. The Historical Prices from 1-Jun-2017 to 31-May-2018 were collected for each of the Stocks.

2. From the Historical Prices gathered in Step 1, the normalized prices of each day for each Stocks were calculated as (Stock Price – Mean(Stock Prices)) / Standard Deviation(Stock Prices).

3. From the normalized prices determined in Step 2, the distance was calculated for each day for each pair by squaring the difference between the normalized prices for the day of each pair.

4. Lastly, the square of the distances determined in Step 3 were summed to find the distance between each pair. This figure is provided in the table below.

	CIL	GMDC	GNRL	ACL	ACPL
GIPCL	552.48	123.18	345.02	288.26	100.93
JPVL	435.14	145.78	425.48	181.98	150.66
JSW	142.16	270.44	680.09	118.87	516.34
NHPC	686.09	328.67	180.44	712.26	242.99
NTPC	412.42	208.79	545.87	148.91	438.62
PGRID	841.18	477.22	278.55	656.26	399.97
RIL	830.04	559.33	201.94	866.16	347.25
SJVN	150.68	248.28	557.56	261.02	408.01

The minimum distance is between GIPCL and ACPL. However, ACPL is not a solvent company. Thus, we will not form this pair.

The second minimum distance is between JSW and ACL. However, ACL is not a solvent company. Thus, we will not form this pair.

The third minimum distance is between GIPCL and GMDC. However, GIPCL already appears in our pair from Power Industry. Thus, we will not form this pair.

The fourth minimum distance is between <u>JSW Energy Ltd</u> and <u>Coal India Ltd</u>. We will form this pair.

6.3.2 ALLOCATING FUNDS TO EACH SHARE

We apply Capital Asset Pricing Model (CAPM). According to CAPM, the risk of investment is measured in β. We gather the β for all the Shares we have selected and then apply Linear Programming to maximize β within the limits as acceptable to the Investor.

A value of 1 for β indicates that the Shares moves along with the market. So, the risk in the Share is that same as the risk in the market.

A value higher than 1 for β indicates that the Share is expected to move higher than the market. This indicates that the Share is riskier than the market. Investing in this Share, we should thus expect higher returns as we are taking additional risk.

If β is less than 0, it indicates that the Share moves in opposite direction of the market.

After discussion with the Investor, it was established that they are ready for a maximum value of 1.6 for β. The values of β is listed below.

Share	β
DLF Ltd	2.24
Titan Company Ltd	1.10
HDFC Ltd	0.86
Hindustan Unilever Ltd	0.65
Tata Consultancy Services Ltd	0.25
ITC Ltd	0.78
JSW Energy Ltd	1.74
Coal India Ltd	0.71
Gujarat Industries Power Company Ltd	1.49
Jaiprakash Power Ventures Ltd	2.29

Initially, we make equal allocation of funds to each of the Shares.

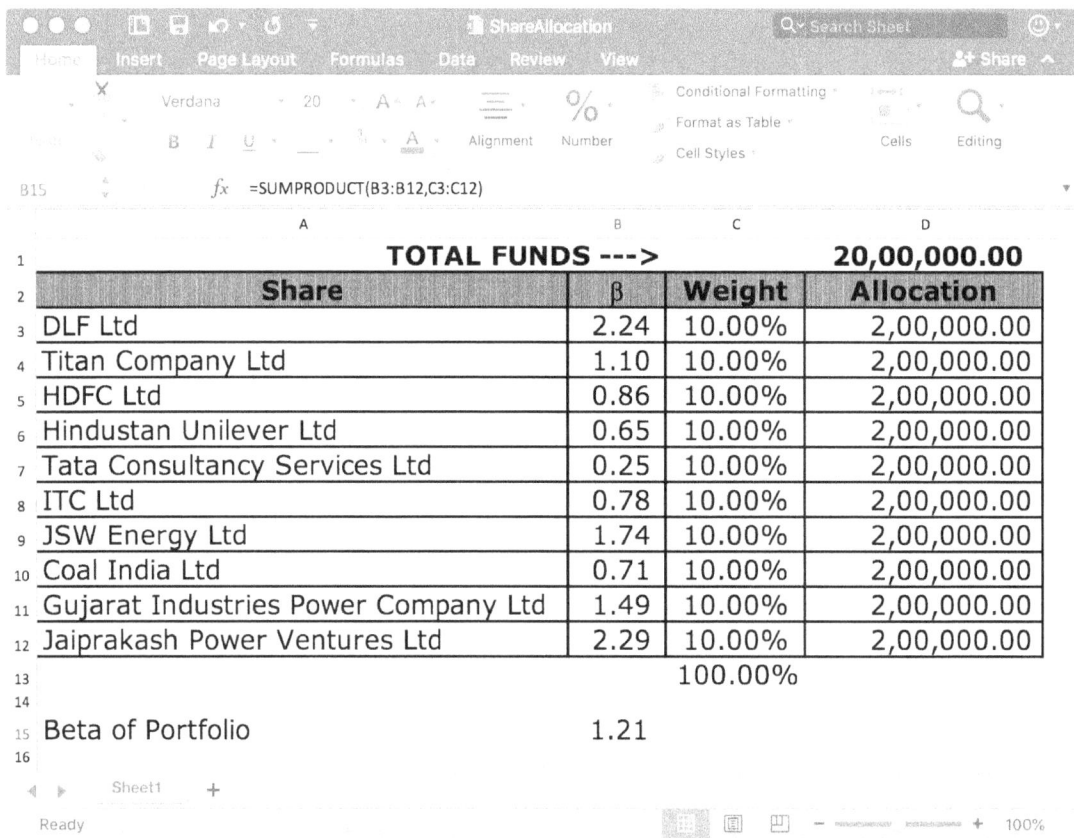

Share	β	Weight	Allocation
TOTAL FUNDS --->			20,00,000.00
DLF Ltd	2.24	10.00%	2,00,000.00
Titan Company Ltd	1.10	10.00%	2,00,000.00
HDFC Ltd	0.86	10.00%	2,00,000.00
Hindustan Unilever Ltd	0.65	10.00%	2,00,000.00
Tata Consultancy Services Ltd	0.25	10.00%	2,00,000.00
ITC Ltd	0.78	10.00%	2,00,000.00
JSW Energy Ltd	1.74	10.00%	2,00,000.00
Coal India Ltd	0.71	10.00%	2,00,000.00
Gujarat Industries Power Company Ltd	1.49	10.00%	2,00,000.00
Jaiprakash Power Ventures Ltd	2.29	10.00%	2,00,000.00
		100.00%	
Beta of Portfolio	1.21		

The Linear Programming Problem is setup as follows.

Set Objective: $B$15

To: ○ Max   Min   Value Of:

By Changing Variable Cells:

$C$3:$C$12

Subject to the Constraints:

$B$15 <= 1.6	Add
$C$10 <= 0.2	
$C$11 <= 0.2	Change
$C$12 <= 0.2	
$C$13 = 1	
$C$3 <= 0.2	Delete
$C$4 <= 0.2	
$C$5 <= 0.2	
$C$6 <= 0.2	Reset All
$C$7 <= 0.2	
$C$8 <= 0.2	Load/Save

☑ Make Unconstrained Variables Non-Negative

Select a Solving Method: GRG Nonlinear ▼   Options

Solving Method

Select the GRG Nonlinear engine for Solver Problems that are smooth nonlinear. Select the LP Simplex engine for linear Solver Problems, and select the Evolutionary engine for Solver problems that are non-smooth.

Close   Solve

The Final Allocation is as follows.

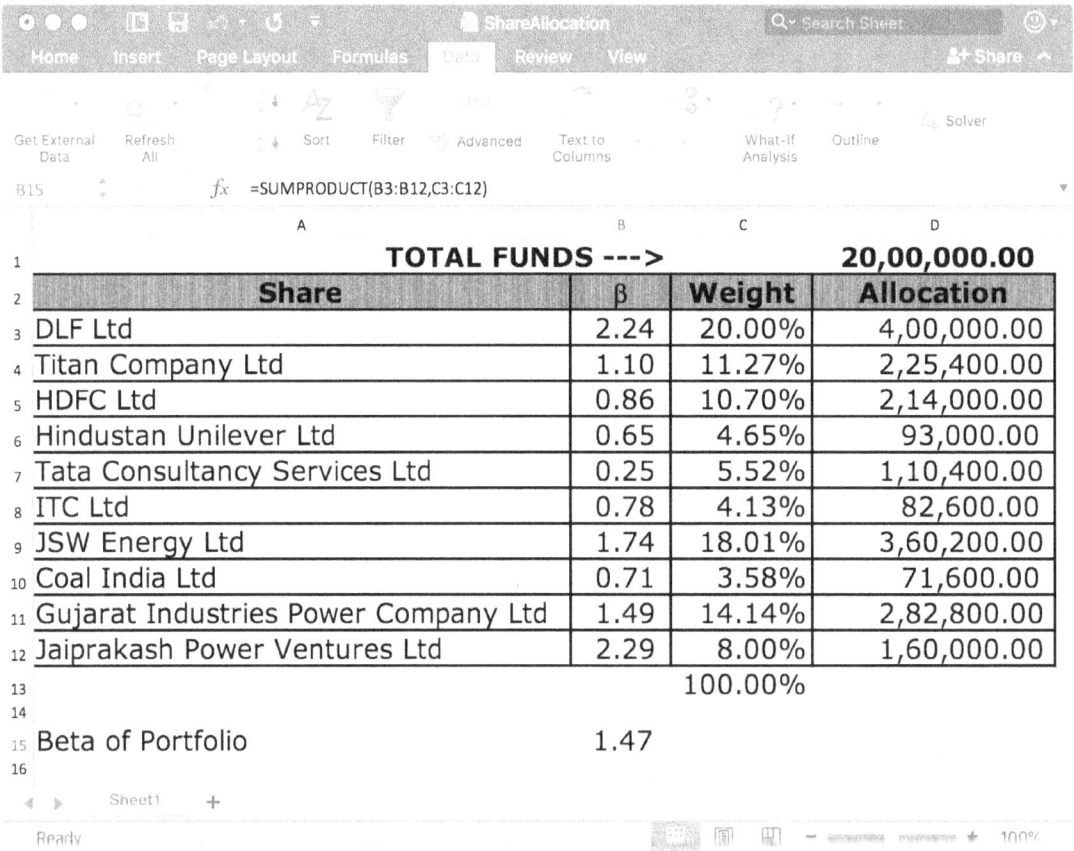

So, we decide the allocation in Shares as follows.

Share	Funds	Current Market Price	Possible Number of Shares
DLF Ltd (DLF)	Rs. 4,00,000	198.35	2,017
Titan Company Ltd (Titan)	Rs. 2,25,400	900.00	250
HDFC Ltd (HDFC)	Rs. 2,14,000	1826.50	117
Hindustan Unilever Ltd (HUL)	Rs. 93,000	1623.50	57
Tata Consultancy Services Ltd (TCS)	Rs. 1,10,400	1841.20	60
ITC Ltd (ITC)	Rs. 82,600	264.85	312
JSW Energy Ltd (JSWE)	Rs. 3,60,200	70.65	5,098
Coal India Ltd (CIL)	Rs. 71,600	275.30	260
Gujarat Industries Power Company Ltd (GIPCL)	Rs. 2,82,800	92.00	3,074
Jaiprakash Power Ventures Ltd (JPPV)	Rs. 1,60,000	3.25	49,231

Note that JSW Energy Ltd and Coal India Ltd are pairs. So, we must consider the sum of their allocation for trading in this pair.

We study the performance possible from this portfolio of Shares.

From www.economictimes.com, I have gathered the historical

returns from the selected shares. The calculation from these figures

is provided below. *(**For calculating Sharpe Ratio and Treynor**

Ratio, we consider Risk Free Rate as 7.10%)*

Share	RETURNS (%)			E_r (%)	σ (%)	Sharpe Ratio	Treynor Ratio
	1 yr	3 yr	5 yr				
DLF	3.98	86.77	5.80	32.18	47.28	0.53	0.11
Titan	73.12	150.03	300.45	174.53	115.63	1.45	1.52
HDFC	11.41	50.84	118.82	60.36	54.33	0.98	0.62
HUL	45.88	86.80	170.30	100.99	63.41	1.48	1.44
TCS	51.86	44.80	152.79	83.15	60.41	1.26	3.04
ITC	-12.50	31.53	20.01	13.01	22.83	0.26	0.08
JSWE	12.96	-26.97	47.64	11.21	37.34	0.11	0.02
CIL	7.94	-30.39	-9.40	-10.62	19.19	-0.92	-0.25
GIPCL	-12.05	13.73	31.92	11.20	22.09	0.19	0.03
JPPV	-24.18	-49.53	-85.45	-53.05	30.79	-1.95	-0.26
EXPECTED PORTFOLIO RETURNS				41.37			
PORTFOLIO RISK (σ)					28.60		
PORTFOLIO SHARPE RATIO						1.20	
PORTFOLIO TREYNOR RATIO							0.23

The diversification can be studied from the correlations between the

Shares. They are as follows.

	DLF	Titan	HDFC	HUL	TCS	ITC	JSWE	CIL	GIPCL	JPPV
DLF										
Titan	-0.16									
HDFC	-0.13	1.00								
HUL	-0.17	1.00	1.00							
TCS	-0.53	0.92	0.91	0.93						
ITC	0.72	0.57	0.60	0.56	0.21					
JSWE	-0.88	0.62	0.59	0.63	0.87	-0.29				
CIL	-0.90	-0.28	-0.31	-0.27	0.11	-0.95	0.58			
GIPCL	0.12	0.96	0.97	0.96	0.78	0.78	0.37	-0.54		
JPPV	0.08	-1.00	-1.00	-1.00	-0.64	-0.64	-0.55	0.36	-0.98	

7 FINAL RECOMMENDATION

The final recommendation from this analysis is that the company should invest its Rs. 50,00,000 as follows to get an expected return of at least 18% per annum in five years.

Instrument	Amount (Rs.)
Fixed Deposits	**Rs. 10,00,000**
HDFC Bank Ltd	Rs. 2,60,000
Ananda Cooperative Bank	Rs. 1,10,000
Gnana Shale Souharda Cooperative Bank	Rs. 6,30,000
Mutual Funds	**Rs. 20,00,000**
HDFC Index Fund NIFTY Plan	Rs. 5,00,000
SBI Dynamic Bond Fund	Rs. 1,60,000
Axis Long Term Equity Fund	Rs. 5,00,000
Franklin India Bluechip Fund	Rs. 3,40,000
Aditya Birla SL Frontline Equity Fund	Rs. 5,00,000
Shares	**Rs. 20,00,000**
DLF Ltd	Rs. 4,00,000
Titan Company Ltd	Rs. 2,25,400
HDFC Ltd	Rs. 2,14,000
Hindustan Unilever Ltd	Rs. 93,000
Tata Consultancy Services Ltd	Rs. 1,10,400
ITC Ltd	Rs. 82,600
JSW Energy Ltd	Rs. 3,60,200
Coal India Ltd	Rs. 71,600
Gujarat Industries Power Company Ltd	Rs. 2,82,800
Jaiprakash Power Ventures Ltd	Rs. 1,60,000

The Investor needs staying invested in the Fixed Deposits and Mutual Funds for five years or more.

In case of the Shares, the Investor need staying invested in the following shares for 1 year before changing the portfolio- DLF Ltd, Titan Company Ltd, HDFC Ltd, Hindustan Unilever Ltd, Tata Consultancy Services Ltd, ITC Ltd. The remaining four shares combination needs changing after six months.

8 APPENDIX I – Annual Reports Studied

The Annual Reports of the following Companies were studied in preparing this report.

Sl.	Company
1.	ACC Ltd
2.	Apollo Tyres Ltd
3.	Auroma Coke Ltd
4.	Austral Coke & Projects Ltd
5.	Avenue Supermarts Ltd
6.	Axis Bank Ltd
7.	Bajaj Finance Ltd
8.	Bajaj Finserv Ltd
9.	Bank of Baroda Ltd
10.	Bharat Electronics Ltd
11.	Bharat Forge Ltd
12.	Bharti Airtel Ltd
13.	Biocon Ltd
14.	Canara Bank Ltd
15.	Capital First Ltd
16.	Castrol India Ltd
17.	Chambal Fertilisers and Chemicals Ltd
18.	Coal India Ltd
19.	Cummins India Ltd
20.	Cyient Ltd
21.	Dabur India Ltd
22.	Deepak Nitrate Ltd
23.	DLF Ltd
24.	Dr. Reddy Laboratories Ltd
25.	Federal Bank Ltd
26.	Granules India Ltd
27.	Gruh Finance Ltd
28.	Gujarat Industries Power Company Ltd
29.	Gujarat Mineral Development Corporation Ltd
30.	Gujarat Natural Resources Ltd
31.	HCL Technologies Ltd
32.	HDFC Bank Ltd
33.	HDFC Ltd
34.	Hindustan Petroleum Corp Ltd
35.	Hindustan Unilever Ltd
36.	ICICI Bank Ltd
37.	India Cements Ltd
38.	Infosys Ltd
39.	ITC Ltd
40.	Jain Irrigation Systems Ltd
41.	Jaiprakash Power Ventures Ltd
42.	Jet Airways Ltd
43.	Jindal Steel & Power Ltd
44.	JSW Energy Ltd
45.	JSW Steel Ltd

46.	Just Dial Ltd
47.	Karnataka Bank Ltd
48.	Kiri Industries Ltd
49.	Kotak Mahindra Bank Ltd
50.	Larsen & Toubro Ltd
51.	LG Balakrishna & Bros Ltd
52.	LIC Housing Finance Ltd
53.	Magma Fincorp Ltd
54.	Mahindra & Mahindra Ltd
55.	Maruti Suzuki India Ltd
56.	Minda Corporation Ltd
57.	MindTree Ltd
58.	Motherson Sumi Systems Ltd
59.	National Aluminium Company Ltd
60.	Navin Fluorine International Ltd
61.	NHPC Ltd
62.	NTPC Ltd
63.	Oil India Ltd
64.	Pidilite Industries Ltd
65.	Power Grid Corporation India Ltd
66.	RBL Bank Ltd
67.	REC Ltd
68.	Reliance Industries Ltd
69.	Shree Cement Ltd
70.	Siemens Ltd
71.	Sintex Industries Ltd
72.	SJVN Ltd
73.	State Bank of India Ltd
74.	Supreme Industries Ltd
75.	Suzlon Energy Ltd
76.	Tata Consultancy Services Ltd
77.	Tata Elxsi Ltd
78.	Tata Motors Ltd
79.	Tejas Networks Ltd
80.	Titan Company Ltd
81.	Vedanta Ltd
82.	VIP Industries Ltd
83.	Yes Bank Ltd
84.	Zydus Wellness Ltd

9 APPENDIX II – List of Web Sites Searched

Sl.	Paper
1.	www.economictimes.com
2.	www.moneycontrol.com
3.	www.bseindia.com
4.	www.nseindia.com
5.	www.wikipedia.com

10 APPENDIX III – List of Papers Researched

Sl.	Paper
1.	http://blog.efpsa.org/2013/02/28/how-to-read-and-get-the-most-out-of-a-journal-article/ This paper explains how to read papers on trading strategies.
2.	https://www.chicagobooth.edu/~/media/FE874EE65F624AAEBD0166B1974FD74D.pdf This paper is the original paper by Piotroski (F-Score).
3.	https://www.chicagobooth.edu/pdf/ballbrown1968.pdf This paper is the original paper by Ball & Brown.
4.	http://econ.au.dk/fileadmin/Economics_Business/Education/Summer_University_2012/6308_Advanced_Financial_Accounting/Advanced_Financial_Accounting/2/Sloan_1996_TAR.pdf This paper is the original paper by Sloan.
5.	http://pages.stern.nyu.edu/~lpederse/papers/BettingAgainstBeta.pdf This paper is the original paper by Pedersen and Frazzini.
6.	https://papers.ssrn.com/sol3/papers.cfm?abstract_id=299107 This paper is the original paper by Jagdeesh and Titman.
7.	https://papers.ssrn.com/sol3/papers.cfm?abstract_id=403180 This paper is the original paper by Professor Mohanram (G-Score).
8.	https://www.fidelity.com/viewpoints/guide-to-diversification This paper explains the importance of Diversification.
9.	http://papers.ssrn.com/sol3/papers.cfm?abstract_id=141615 This paper by Gatev, Goetzmann and Rouwenhorst forms the basis for this "Pairs Trading" strategy.
10.	https://blog.wealthfront.com/benchmark-investments-portfolio-performance/ This paper discusses the ways in which one can benchmark one's portfolio performance.

11 BIBLIOGRAPHY

TERM	EXPLANATION
CAPM	The **capital asset pricing model (CAPM)** is a model used to determine a theoretically appropriate required rate of return of an asset, to make decisions about adding assets to a well-diversified portfolio. The model considers the asset's sensitivity to non-diversifiable risk (also known as systematic risk or market risk), often represented by the quantity beta (β) in the financial industry, as well as the expected return of the market and the expected return of a theoretical risk-free asset. CAPM assumes a particular form of utility functions (in which only first and second moments matter, that is risk is measured by variance, for example a quadratic utility) or alternatively asset returns whose probability distributions are completely described by the first two moments (for example, the normal distribution) and zero transaction costs (necessary for diversification to get rid of all idiosyncratic risk). Under these conditions, CAPM shows that the cost of equity capital is determined only by beta. Despite it failing numerous empirical tests, and the existence of more modern approaches to asset pricing and portfolio selection (such as arbitrage pricing theory and Merton's portfolio problem), the CAPM still remains popular due to its simplicity and utility in a variety of situations.
F-Score	**Piotroski F-Score** is a number between 0-9 which is used to assess strength of company's financial position. The Score is used by financial investors to find the best value stocks (nine being the best). The Score is named after Stanford Accounting Professor, Joseph Piotroski.
Fixed Deposit	A **fixed deposit (FD)** is a financial instrument provided by banks or NBFCs (Non-Banking Financial Company) which provides investors a higher rate of interest than a regular savings account, until the given maturity date. It may or may not require the creation of a separate account. It is known as a term deposit or time deposit in Canada, Australia, New Zealand, and the US, and as a bond in the United Kingdom and India. They are very safe investments. Term deposits in India, Nepal, and Pakistan are used to denote a larger class of investments with varying levels of liquidity. The defining criterion for a fixed deposit is that the money cannot be withdrawn from the FD as compared to a recurring deposit or a demand deposit before maturity. Some banks may offer additional services to FD holders such as loans against FD certificates at competitive interest rates. It's important to note that banks may offer lesser interest rates under uncertain economic conditions. The interest rate varies between 4 and 7.25 percent. The tenure of an FD can vary from 7, 15 or 45 days to 1.5 years and can be as high as 10 years. These investments are safer than Post Office Schemes as they are covered by the Deposit Insurance and Credit Guarantee Corporation (DICGC). However, DICGC guarantees amount up to ₹ 100,000 (about $1555) per depositor per bank. They also offer income tax and wealth tax benefits.

Mutual Fund	A **mutual fund** is a professionally managed investment fund that pools money from many investors to purchase securities. These investors may be retail or institutional in nature.
	Mutual funds have advantages and disadvantages compared to direct investing in individual securities. The primary advantages of mutual funds are that they provide economies of scale, a higher level of diversification, they provide liquidity, and they are managed by professional investors. On the negative side, investors in a mutual fund must pay various fees and expenses.
Share	Corporations issue shares which are offered for sale to raise share capital. The owner of shares in the corporation is a shareholder (or stockholder) of the corporation. A share is an indivisible unit of capital, expressing the ownership relationship between the company and the shareholder. The denominated value of a share is its face value, and the total of the face value of issued shares represent the capital of a company, which may not reflect the market value of those shares.
	The income received from the ownership of shares is a dividend. The process of purchasing and selling shares often involves going through a stockbroker as a middleman. There are different types of shares such as equity shares, preference shares, bonus shares, right shares, employees stock option plans and sweat equity shares.
Sharpe Ratio	The **Sharpe Ratio** (also known as the Sharpe Index, the Sharpe Measure, and the reward-to-variability ratio) is a way to examine the performance of an investment by adjusting for its risk. The ratio measures the excess return (or risk premium) per unit of deviation in an investment asset or a trading strategy, typically referred to as risk, named after William F. Sharpe.
Treynor Ratio	The **Treynor Ratio** (sometimes called the reward-to-volatility ratio or Treynor Measure), named after Jack L. Treynor, is a measurement of the returns earned in excess of that which could have been earned on an investment that has no diversifiable risk (e.g., Treasury bills or a completely diversified portfolio), per each unit of market risk assumed.
	The Treynor ratio relates excess return over the risk-free rate to the additional risk taken; however, systematic risk is used instead of total risk. The higher the Treynor ratio, the better the performance of the portfolio under analysis.

12 About the Author

Partha Majumdar is just a programmer.

Partha has a passion for sharing knowledge. He documents his experiences in technical and management aspects in his blog http://www.parthamajumdar.org. Also, he regularly publishes videos on his YouTube channel - https://www.youtube.com/channel/UCbzrZ_aeyiYVo1WJKhlP5sQ. Partha has developed OLTP systems for Telcos, Hospitals, Tea Gardens, Factories, Travel Houses, Cricket tournaments, etc. Since 2012, Partha has been developing Data Products and intensively working on Machine Learning and Deep Learning. Partha has a panache for finding patterns in most of what he gets involved in. As a result, Partha has been helpful to teams in developing Rapid Development Tools.

Partha has continued to learn new domains and technology throughout his career. After graduating in Mathematics, Partha completed a master's in Telecommunications, a master's in Computer Security, and a master's in Information Technology. He has also completed two Executive MBAs in Information Systems and Business Analytics. He completed a PG Certificate program in AI/ML/DL from Manipal Academy of Higher Education (Dubai), an advanced certificate in Cyber Security from IIT (Kanpur), and a PG-level advanced certificate in Computational Data Sciences from IISc (Bengaluru). He is pursuing a Doctorate in Business Administration from the Swiss School of Business and Management (Geneva).

13 Books by the Author

13.1 Learn Emotion Analysis with R

This book covers how to conduct Emotion Analysis based on Lexicons. Through a detailed code walkthrough, the book will explain how to develop Sentiment and Emotion Analysis systems from popular data sources, including WhatsApp, Twitter, etc.

The book starts with a discussion on R and Shiny programming, as these will lay the foundation for the system to be developed for Emotion Analysis. Then, the book discusses the essentials of Sentiment Analysis and Emotion Analysis. The book then proceeds to build Shiny applications for Emotion Analysis. The book rounds off by creating a tool for Emotion Analysis from the data obtained from Twitter and WhatsApp.

Emotion Analysis can also be performed using Machine Learning. However, this requires labeled data. This is a logical next step after reading this book.

Link in Amazon.com Store: https://www.amazon.com/dp/B096K2SVF2

13.2 Linear Programming for Project Management Professionals

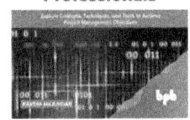

This book assists project management professionals in resolving project crashing situations through linear programming. It demonstrates how the PM team can help streamline the project's on-time completion and cost optimization.

The book begins with an understanding of project management processes and frameworks such as WBS, PDM, and EVM. The book helps build familiarity with the PM team's project monitoring procedures. It helps investigate linear programming problems (LPPs) and the mathematical foundations for their formulation. It covers various approaches to solving the LPP, including graphical methods, their limitations, and the necessity of tools such as MS Excel's Solver. It also covers how the PM team can solve LPP with the help of Solver.

This book covers various business and technical scenarios for crashing a project. It teaches how to formulate the problem of optimizing a project for time and cost using LPP. This book then discusses how LPP can be solved using Solver and more complex issues. It also explores the relationship between earned value management and crashing a project.

Link in Amazon.com Store: https://www.amazon.com/dp/B09PD1GFMY

13.3 Mastering Classification Algorithms for Machine Learning

Classification algorithms are essential in machine learning as they allow us to predict the class or category of input by considering its features. These algorithms significantly impact multiple applications like spam filtering, sentiment analysis, image recognition, and fraud detection.

The book starts with an introduction to problem-solving in machine learning and subsequently focuses on classification problems. It then explores the Naïve Bayes algorithm, a probabilistic method widely used in industrial applications. The application of the Bayes Theorem and underlying assumptions in developing the Naïve Bayes algorithm for classification is also covered. Moving forward, the book focuses on the Logistic Regression algorithm, exploring the sigmoid function and its significance in binary classification. The book also covers Decision Trees and discusses the Gini Factor, Entropy, and their use in splitting trees and generating decision leaves. The Random Forest algorithm is also thoroughly explained as a cutting-edge method for classification.

Link in Amazon.com Store: https://www.amazon.com/dp/935551851X

13.4 Gartner Research Analysis

Gartner Hype-Cycle Report has a lot of information about new Inventions and Innovations. Apart from the details of the inventions and innovations, it also states the companies working on these technologies and their stage in getting their products ready for commercialization. It can be overwhelming to go through the details of this report.

This book systematically states a mechanism for using the Gartner Hype-Cycle report to draw valuable inferences. The mechanism is explained through a live case study. It shows how to narrow down the provided options for a given objective. Any such research will only be complete with a detailed analysis of the narrowed-down options by studying more material outside the report. The illustrated mechanism can be used as a precursor for using the Gartner Hype-Cycle report.

Link in Amazon.com Store: https://www.amazon.com/dp/B0CK582Y2M

13.5 Creating an Investment Portfolio

Investing is an essential requirement whether one is an individual or a corporation. If the right investment decisions are made, it can be fulfilling for the investor. Making the right decisions in investment is a scientific process. So, it is essential to understand the involved theories and their applications.

This book discusses portfolio creation's essential theories and applications, including fixed deposits, mutual funds, and shares. The discussion includes the needed mathematics. Also, simple and omnipresent tools that can be used for the calculations are illustrated.

This book will be helpful for both individual investors and companies.

Link in Amazon.com Store: https://www.amazon.com/dp/B0CK99SPKZ

13.6 Weekend in Jordan

We planned a trip to Jordan to celebrate our 20th marriage anniversary. It was a last-minute plan, with tickets being purchased and bookings made just about a week before the travel. This was possible because Jordan provides visa-on-arrival for Indians. Jordan also provides visa-on-arrival for nationals of many countries. So, such a trip will be possible for many people worldwide.

The trip turned out to be quite an adventure for us. For a weekend, we felt like we were in a movie. That has made the trip etched in our memories. Jordan is beautiful and is a wonderful country to explore. Being a relatively small country, exploring most of Jordan during the weekend is possible.

The book details our findings in Petra, the Dead Sea, and Amman.

Link in Amazon.com Store: https://www.amazon.com/dp/B0CK5N6B3W

13.7 Elephant Ride in Chang Wangpo

Thailand welcomed ~11.5 million tourists in 2022. In 2020, tourism accounted for ~6% of the Thai GDP. We had lived in Bangkok between 1996 and 1999. When another opportunity to visit Thailand came our way in 2018, we grabbed it.

Many things have changed in Thailand since our last stay. For example, traffic in Bangkok used to be a nightmare. On one occasion in 1996, I had waited at a traffic signal for ~45 minutes. Now, Bangkok has an efficient metro system, which has made getting to places very comfortable. Most of the good things we had enjoyed earlier are still in place. Getting to places outside Bangkok was never a challenge, as the road network is beautiful. This has only improved. The number of attractions has increased. And, of course, Thais are lovely people.

This was a business trip that overlapped with our 26th marriage anniversary. So, we decided to celebrate in Thailand while doing the needed business. During this trip, we revisited some places in Bangkok and Kanchanaburi. The surprise for us was the trip to Chang Wangpo, a once-in-a-lifetime experience

Link in Amazon.com Store: https://www.amazon.com/dp/B0CKGWH97S

13.8 Weekend in South Sikkim

South Sikkim has several interesting places to visit. Generally, tourists to Sikkim explore places in North Sikkim like Gangtok, Nathu La Pass, Pelling, Yumthang Valley, etc. This book details what could be found in South Sikkim.

We pass through Gangtok, Nathu La Pass, Tsomgo Lake, Baba Ka Mandir, Namchi, Char Dham, Samdruptse Monastery, Temi Tea Gardens, Yangang, and Bengal Safari in Siliguri (West Bengal).

Link in Amazon.com Store: https://www.amazon.com/dp/B0CKL1DNTJ